Feast Day
COOKBOOK

Feast Day COOKBOOK

by *KATHERINE BURTON*

& *HELMUT RIPPERGER*

Catholic Authors Press

2005

Designed by
ALANSON HEWES

Manufactured
in the
UNITED STATES OF AMERICA

Contents

CONTENTS

Introduction

The celebrations surrounding festival days are a definite part of our Christian tradition. "We have received these days by tradition from our forefathers," says Saint Augustine, "and we transmit them to those that follow to be celebrated with like devotion."

Saint Augustine refers, of course, mainly to the religious observance of feast days, but the custom of gathering together for a meal after the ceremonies and the processions, the prayers and the devotions, of offering thanksgiving for divine favors and sharing the warmth of home and hearth in the name of God is in the ancient and honorable usage of centuries. It would be impossible to find a land where there is no such celebration of holy days, where families and friends do not gather to honor events in the life of Our Lord, such as His birth at Christmas or His Resurrection at Easter, or feasts of the Blessed Virgin or the saints in heaven. And in many countries the homeless and the stranger are bidden to the holiday board, or a portion of food is set aside for the poor and the needy, later to be taken to them.

The meals prepared in every land on these occasions include traditional dishes, made from recipes handed down for generations, and sometimes the entire meal is prescribed by custom, often its least detail being symbolic in meaning. For example, in Poland the Christmas Eve meal or *Wigilia* is strictly ordered—in setting, in number of courses and dishes, and in the kinds and mixtures of food. The same is true of the Polish Easter *Swiecone*, or Blessed Meal; and similar customs prevail on these days in other Slavic countries. In France we have the traditional *Réveil-*

lon after Midnight Mass on Christmas, and in Italy the *Cenone*, or Christmas Eve supper.

Again, the food for a festal day or season may be very simple. There are traditions concerning fasting as well as feasting, and for certain days only one time-honored or appropriate dish is known.

It is interesting to note how many of the recipes for special occasions have to do with bread and cakes. This comes from the universal reverence for bread as the basic food of mankind. For example in Hungary, the sign of the Cross is made over the loaf of newly baked bread before it is touched, and all members of the household stand as the first piece is cut by the head of the family. Should a bit of bread drop to the floor and someone step upon it, that person must pick it up and kiss it.

Breads and cakes and cookies—the Russian Easter *Koulich*, the Good Friday Hot Cross Bun of England, the Christmas *Lebkuchen* of Germany, the Shrove Tuesday pancakes and doughnuts of many countries—their recipes are legion. We have included many of these, but there are hundreds of others which space does not permit, so many in fact that one large volume could be devoted to them alone.

It must be borne in mind that some Christian festival observances spring from former pagan feasts, for which the primitive Church found a counterpart to draw the people from other allegiances to its own. Pagan feasts in honor of the earth, the coming of spring, the reaping of the harvest, were given a Christian connotation; the ancient fire and water worship of pagan times became the blessing of water and the lighting of fires in Christian worship. Even the old names have often remained in certain languages: in English the word Easter is from the name of the Anglo-Saxon goddess Oestre, and Lent comes from the Anglo-Saxon word *Lencten*, meaning spring. Once the goddess Flora was honored in May; today for Christians this is the month of the Blessed Virgin. Easter eggs and Christmas trees go far back into antiquity—the tree perhaps to Druid days, the colored eggs to ancient Persia and Egypt.

The barbaric and cruel practices that marked many of the pagan observances have gone, but some superstitious elements remain, and in many countries have been added to by folklore and customs of peasant and local origin. Because of their intrinsic interest we have noted many of these local customs in reference to diversions and food. We have included too some almost forgotten Christian feast days once of great importance, as Michaelmas, Martinmas, and Lammas Day. Then also we have given dishes traditional to the feasts of, or suggested by incidents in the lives of the saints, as well as well-known national dishes of a country, eaten on its patronal feast, as Saint George's Day in England, Saint Andrew's in Scotland, Saint David's in Wales. The reader will note that we have even permitted ourselves an occasional pleasantry, such as Fruit Cobbler on the feast of the patron of shoemakers, or Lost Bread on the feast of Saint Anthony. We assure him that our aim was not to shock but to divert.

With the exception of the American Independence Day and Thanksgiving, we have treated only the feast days of the Church. Many of these have been omitted either because they did not lend themselves to traditions in the matter of food, or because any such collection as this must necessarily stop somewhere. We are ourselves most keenly aware of its limitations and many omissions.

Perhaps we should add that we are also aware the liturgical year begins with Advent, but that for the convenience of all we have followed the usual calendar, beginning with January 1st. And as some may question our placing of a movable feast, such as Whitsunday, Shrove Tuesday, or Easter, in a given month, we may explain that we have listed these only approximately where they occur and have included a Table of Movable Feasts at the end of this book so that the reader may find the exact dates of these feasts for a good many years to come.

It may also be well to add a reminder that the feasts of the Eastern Orthodox Church follow the Julian calendar and not our own, the Gregorian. Thus when we speak in our book of the Russian Easter on the same date as that celebrated in the West, we refer to the celebration rather than to the date.

In some countries today the observance of Christian feasts is forbidden. We remember that it has been forbidden before, as the Puritans once forbade in our own country the celebration of Christmas. The feast days flourish again as time passes; the roots are alive; the plants will bud and bloom once more. Therefore we do not speak of these customs as in the past, but merely as temporarily interrupted—perhaps not always entirely interrupted. Did our newspapers not carry but recently the account of crowds in Russia flocking into churches and cathedrals, bringing their Easter food to be blessed? . . .

And now, a word about the recipes themselves. They have been gathered from the four corners of the earth and, in point of time, several go back to the biblical era, while others range through the centuries down to modern times. We have not attempted to standardize them in any way, preferring to keep the flavor of their original compilation. However, as given here, all of them are practical and adapted to present day cookery. A possible exception is Scripture Cake, but even this can be successfully made by anyone having a practical knowledge of baking. And finally, these recipes can be used not only for feast days, but for every day. Recalling that seventeen hundred years ago, the Greek author Athenaeus wrote, "A change of meat is often good, and those who are wearied of common food take new pleasure in a novel meal," we offer them as a refreshing change from routine meals and for the delectation as well as interest of both cook and diner.

It is always a pleasant task to acknowledge indebtedness for favors and inspiration received. Obviously the authors of this book cannot single out each and every one who has shown interest in its preparation by giving practical and helpful aid and advice. A selected check list of reference material for further reading will be found at the end of the book, in which we acknowledge many of the sources of our information. However, we do wish to express our particular gratitude to Mrs. F. Dodd McHugh and the Sisters of the Holy Family of Nazareth, Torresdale, Pennsylvania, for information on Polish feast day customs and recipes; to Dr. Lili Gonde for data included in the French sections of the book; and to the Reverend Claiborne Lafferty of the North American College in Rome for a useful list of Italian festival dishes; to Mrs. Marian Tracy, and to the Bronxville Public Library.

And a lion's share of appreciation and thanks should go to the New York Public Library. It would be simple to set down the names of the various heads of departments who have given so generously of their time, but we feel that to do so adequately and fairly, we should rightly commence the list with the names of the Messers Astor, Lenox, and Tilden. However, we feel that the "heads" have often been given their due praise in print in the past. We would like to thank here the hundreds who through the years have prepared the millions of cards that make up the general catalogue of the Library; the patient attendants who took and safely forwarded the many call slips we made out day after day in the course of our research; the unseen and unknown (to us, at least) workers in the underground stacks, who found the books we asked for; and, finally, the pages who so swiftly sought us out and brought the needed treasures to us.

K. B.

August 10, 1951 *H. R.*

Feast Day
COOKBOOK

JANUARY 1

New Year's Day

FAR BACK in time goes the celebration of the first day of the New Year, back to the time of the Druids, when priests brought from the sacred wood mistletoe boughs to distribute to the people. In ancient Rome sacrifices were offered to Janus, the god for whom the month was named—a god with two faces, looking both into the past and into the future. Presents were exchanged on this day, and in time these became very elaborate indeed. Christian emperors allowed the pleasant custom to continue, but so many idolatrous rites remained attached to the celebration that at last the Church prohibited its members from observing it in any way.

Then when, some centuries later December 25th was fixed upon as the day of the Nativity of Christ, the first of January became a Christian feast day in honor of the Circumcision of Our Lord. But secular customs in connection with the beginning of the New Year continued to overshadow in many places the religious observance of the feast, and much revelry was connected with it. The Middle Ages eagerly seized upon any event that afforded a reasonable excuse for a banquet or feasting—coronations, great victories, and Church festivals. When on "Newyere Daie" in medieval England the country folk after copious repasts drank each other's health in cups of wassail, they afterwards went out to the orchards and "wassailed the trees."

Wassail Bowl

nutmeg	4 glasses sherry
ginger root	3 slices lemon
1 lb. sugar	4 slices toast
3 qts. warm beer	

Grate a little nutmeg and some ginger root over one pound of sugar and add one quart of the beer. Add the sherry and the lemon slices and finally the rest of the beer. Stir, taste, and add more sugar if necessary. Serve in a bowl and float the toast on top.

In England the celebration has always been elaborate and various cakes were made especially for this day. First among them came the seed cake, but the "god cakes" of Coventry were also very popular. These last were of all sizes, some so small they sold for a penny and some so large they sold for a pound, and they were not really cakes at all, but a sort of tart with a filling and cut in a triangle. At St. Albans cakes were made in the form of a woman and were called locally "pope ladies," but neither legend nor history tell why.

God Cakes

1/4 cup butter	1/2 teaspoon nutmeg
1/4 cup sugar	1/4 teaspoon allspice
3/4 cup currants	puff paste or pie dough
1/3 cup lemon peel	

Mix the butter and sugar thoroughly, and add the currants, lemon peel, and spices. Heat in a double boiler for a few minutes and then allow the filling to cool before using. Make a puff paste (or use your richest pie dough) and roll out 1/4 inch thick and cut into 3-inch squares. Place a teaspoon of the filling in one corner of each square. Moisten the edges of the pastry and fold over from corner to corner to make a triangle; seal the edges with a fork. Bake at 450° F. for 10 minutes. Reduce the heat to 350° F. and bake for an additional 10 minutes or until brown.

We read that on this day Queen Elizabeth collected many gifts, a royal custom which sometimes was hard on her subjects, for each strove to outdo the other to win her favor, and she collected such rich offerings as caskets studded with jewels, bracelets, and mantles. But she received simpler gifts as well. There is a record of a box of foreign sweetmeats given her by her physician, ginger candy and lozenges from her apothecary, a box of green ginger from a friend, and "Mrs. Morgan brought a box of cherries and one of apricocks."

The lesser folk in Elizabeth's reign received gifts of gilt nutmegs and pomanders—an apple or an orange—"stıkt round about with cloaves." These ingenious affairs were often hung in milady's room and sometimes put inside wine vessels to preserve wine from "foystiness." The name pomander was originally applied to a small case of silver which contained various aromatic scents. Here is a good way to make a pomander in our day.

Pomander

Take a small, thin-skinned orange and stick whole cloves into it until the surface is entirely studded. Roll the orange in powdered orrisroot and powdered cinnamon, patting on as much as you can. Wrap in tissue paper and put it away for several weeks. Remove the paper, shake off the surplus powder, and the pomander is ready for use. It can be hung up by a ribbon in a closet where it will retain its fragrance and aroma for years.

In France the *Nouvel An* has always been a day when gifts are exchanged rather than on Christmas Day, and at family parties children and grown folk exchange *étrennes.*

In Italy, although the children are given their toys at Epiphany, adults receive their presents at the *Capo d'Anno.*

In the United States New Year's Day has come to mean open house, a day when people pay calls to wish each other joy in the days to come and good fortune for the whole year. In many minds the beverage associated with the day has become fixed, and eggnog is its name. It is, for some, a very heavy drink—imbibing one is possible but two may well prove overwhelming. However, there are beverages for New Year's Day that hail from other lands and which surely would please one's guests. There is, for example, the Swedish *Glögg.*

Glögg

1/3 cup almonds	2 bottles sherry
1 cup raisins	2 bottles port
10 whole cloves	1 cup lump sugar
10 cardamons	1 bottle cognac

6 pieces stick cinnamon

A week before you wish to use your *glögg,* place the almonds (blanched and shredded), the raisins, the cloves, whole cardamons, and the stick cinnamon in a saucepan with enough wine to cover. Place over low heat and bring to just the boiling point. Place in a jar and keep in a cool place. To make your *glögg,* add the rest of the wine to the spiced foundation and heat it in an attractive kettle, chafing dish, or *brûlot* bowl. Bring to the boiling point but do *not* allow it to boil. In a sieve placed over the kettle or bowl, put your lump sugar and slowly pour the bottle of cognac over it, and set it aflame with a match. When the sugar has melted through, the *glögg* is ready. It should be served hot.

With this one might well serve a modern version of the English seed cake.

Seed Cake

1 cup butter	¼ teaspoon salt
5 egg yolks	¾ cup milk
1½ cups sugar	2 teaspoons caraway seeds
3 egg whites	1 teaspoon vanilla
3 cups pastry flour	

3 teaspoons baking powder

Beat the butter until creamy and add the egg yolks and sugar, beating thoroughly. Stir in the egg whites and mix briskly. Sift flour, baking powder, and salt and add to the mixture, alternating with the milk. Beat well; add caraway seeds and vanilla. Pour into a well-greased tube pan and bake at 350° F. for an hour and fifteen minutes. An early American recipe says, "Wash the butter in rose water, drean out the water and add a few drops of oyl of sinnamont."

And here is a cake which could well be made for the New Year, for it is good to eat and also good to consider, especially in these days when the Bible is not so much read as it once was. No doubt many an early American would not have had to look up these references, but for many today it may serve the double purpose of supplying gustatory and religious information.

Scripture Cake

(1) Four and one half cups of III Kings, iv, 22; (2) one and one half cups of Judges v, 25; (3) two cups of Jeremias vi, 20; (4) two cups of I Kings, xxx, 12; (5) two cups of Nahum iii, 12; (6) one cup of Numbers xvii, 8; (7) two tablespoons of I Kings, xiv, 25; (8) six articles of Jeremias xvii, 11; (9) a pinch of Leviticus ii, 13; (10) a teaspoon of Amos iv, 5; (11) season to taste with II Paralipomenon, ix, 9; (12) add citron and follow Solomon's advice for making a good boy, Proverbs xxiii, 14, and you will have a good cake. (Douay Bible.)

There are of course households in which the New Year's family reunion and dinner menu are traditional and inviolable. But for those open to suggestion, we offer a dinner built about a central dish of suckling pig, the standard New Year's roast in many European countries. Usually a bright red apple or an orange is put in the pig's snout, although the Hungarian custom is to put in a four leaf clover. Around the pig's pate is often placed a wreath of bay leaves.

Roast Suckling Pig

Clean the pig carefully. Insert a piece of wood into its mouth to keep it open while roasting. Sage and onion dressing is traditional, but you might use a prune-apple stuffing or a sausage stuffing. Stuff your pig, truss and skewer it. Make 4 parallel slits about 3 inches long on each side of the backbone. Place on a rack, sprinkle with salt and freshly ground pepper, brush with melted butter, and dust with flour. Roast for fifteen minutes at 480° F.; then reduce heat to 350° F. and continue roasting, allowing thirty minutes to the pound. If you wish to have the skin soft, baste every fifteen minutes with hot stock; if crisp (and it's better that way), baste with melted butter. When the roast is ready, remove to a hot serving platter. Remove the piece of wood from the mouth, replace with a bright red apple and insert cranberries for eyes. Finally crown with a wreath of bay leaves. The ears and tail have a tendency to burn, so wrap them carefully in buttered paper which should be removed during the last half hour of roasting.

The European side dishes which accompany the New Year's suckling pig are usually heavy and a bit complicated. We would suggest fluffy mashed potatoes covered with finely chopped onions slightly browned in butter, a dish of Brussels sprouts surrounded with braised chestnuts, and a sharp green salad. The dessert might well be an Apple Florentine which hails from seventeenth-century England. According to the old recipe, this was a deep-dish apple pie baked in a huge pewter or Sheffield plate, filled with "good baking apples, sugar and lemon to the very brim." When baked and before serving, the rich crust was taken off and cut into triangular pieces ready to be replaced, but before this was done a full quart of well-spiced ale, "quite hissing hot," was poured over the apples. We might follow the same instructions but substitute hot cider for the ale.

JANUARY 2

Feast of Saint Macarius

In the fourth century when the desert in Egypt sheltered many hermits, happy in their austere lives and their separation from the world, one of the most famous was Macarius the Younger. We are told he was of joyful countenance and, like Saint Francis of Assisi later, he was the friend of birds and animals. One of the most charming of the stories concerning him relates that one day a hyena came to lay before him her blind cub, just born. The saint restored the sight of the young animal, and the next day the grateful mother returned to him carrying in her mouth a fine sheepskin. Of this Macarius made a garment which he wore until he died.

Macarius' fame spread far and wide because of his piety and spiritual knowledge, and many sought him in his desert abode for advice and guidance. He did not become a hermit until the middle of his life. He had been a sugarplum merchant, and that is why he became the patron of pastry cooks and confectioners. His own product, sugarplums, a term once used only for candied fruits, is today a synonym for sweets of any kind.

Sugarplums

2 lbs. confectionery sugar 1 lb. any fruit water

Cover sugar with enough water to dissolve, and let boil to a syrup. Place fruit in a pan and pour syrup over it.

Turn fruit lightly by shaking pan until all parts are coated. Set to cool, and when this is done pour off syrup and set pan on its side so that the liquid may be well drained off. Should be prepared two days in advance so that glaze will form.

In our day sugarplums are more apt to be replaced by glacéed fruits.

Glacéed Fruits

2 cups sugar
⅔ cup water
⅛ teaspoon cream of tartar

Mix sugar, water, and cream of tartar in a small saucepan. Stir until the sugar is dissolved; then cook to 310° F. —crack stage—without stirring. Remove the syrup from the fire to check boiling and place the saucepan in another pan of hot water. Begin dipping into the syrup at once, using pieces of canned pineapple, canned cherries, figs, grapes, dates, pitted prunes. Nut meats may be glacéed in the same fashion. If the candies are dropped on tin, they will not stick.

FIRST MONDAY IN JANUARY

Handsel Monday

The Scotch prefer to celebrate the New Year on the first Monday in January. This day is known in that country as Handsel Monday, a word derived from an Anglo-Saxon phrase meaning a gift given by hand. Especially among rural workers it is a popular holiday. The farmers give them on that morning a huge breakfast of meats both roasted and boiled, with ale and whiskey to wash it down, and a fine cake to follow. Shortbread invariably appears on the table. No work is done on that day, but everyone goes visiting friends after the meal, partly no doubt to show a holiday spirit but doubtless also to work off the heaviness that follows so unusual an intake of food.

Scotch Shortbread

- 1 cup butter
- ½ cup confectionery sugar
- ¼ teaspoon baking powder
- ¼ teaspoon salt
- 2 cups flour

Beat the butter until soft and gradually add the sugar. Sift the flour, baking powder, and salt together and work into the butter mixture with the hands. A tablespoon of vanilla or some freshly ground nutmeg may also be added. Knead the dough well until no cracks appear. Roll it out to the thickness of ¼ inch and cut into squares or any desired shape. Bake on a greased sheet at 375° F. for about twenty minutes.

JANUARY 6

Epiphany or Twelfth Day

Early in January comes a feast celebrated everywhere and variously throughout the Christian world—Epiphany, from the Greek word *Theophania*, meaning the showing forth of God. Because in the West this signified the manifestation of Christ through the Magi after His birth, it is known as the Day of Kings, and it is also commonly called Twelfth Day, since Epiphany occurs that many days after Christmas.

In the East the manifestation of Christ was connected with His baptism in the Jordan and with baptism in general. From the lighted candle held at baptism, it receives another name—the Feast of Lights. The Greek Orthodox hold at Epiphany a ceremony known as the Blessing of the Waters, at which water is blessed and carried home by the worshippers to be placed close to the familiar icons. In the United States this annual ceremony is in some places carried out even more splendidly than in Greece. In New York the Orthodox Metropolitan carries a gold crucifix to the harbor, throws it into the water in the presence of his congregation, and then several divers leap in, each striving to be the first to recover it.

Epiphany Eve is the setting of a tender legend. It is said that the Wise Men on their way to Bethlehem passed an old woman busily cleaning her house. When she learned where they were going, she asked them to wait until she had finished her work so she could go with them. But the Kings said they could not wait; they told her to follow them when she was ready and catch up with them. As she was a careful housekeeper and also took time to prepare a gift to take to the Child, when she finally started on her way, the others were so far ahead that she never found them. Ever since she wanders through the world, seeking the Child so that she may give Him her gift. In Italy, as Befana—a corruption of Epiphany—she leaves gifts at the houses she visits in the hope of finding the Child she seeks. A time-honored Epiphany dainty in Italy is *Cappelletti all' uso di Romagna.*

Cappelletti all' uso di Romagna

(Little Hats in the Manner of the Romans)

1/4 lb. boiled chicken	1 cup flour
1/4 lb. roast veal	1 egg
3 slices prosciutto (Italian ham)	1/4 lb. cottage cheese
	grated lemon peel

nutmeg, allspice, salt

Grind the meat very fine. It is preferable to use prosciutto but ordinary plain ham may be used. Make a highly seasoned mixture with all the other ingredients. The ground meat may be sautéed in a little butter before being added. Make a paste of 1 cup flour and 1 egg (add an extra egg white if you have it): Put the flour on a board, make a hole in the middle and break in the egg. Work it with a fork until it is firm enough to work with the hands. Knead it thoroughly, adding more flour if necessary, until the paste can be rolled out. Roll as thin as possible and cut into rounds about 3 inches in diameter.

Place a spoonful of filling in the middle of each circle of paste, moisten the edges of the paste with finger dipped in water to seal it securely, and fold into little cones or hats. These *cappelletti* should be cooked in chicken broth for about twenty minutes. Usually they are served with the soup, but sometimes they are served separately with *Mostarda di Cremona.* The Italians say of it, "this is a mustard which is not," for it is made of pieces of fruit, mustard, and spices.

In some lands long ago, children set out to meet the three Kings with cakes and figs, and hay for the camels; in our day in some countries they still take their gifts to the church and lay them before the altar rail.

One charming story goes like this: When Mary heard the tramping feet of the camels, she picked her baby up and held him close, fearing that someone had come to take him from her. And so the Wise Men found them exactly as they had been foretold. When they went home again, the story continues, they resigned their high offices and estates and went forth to teach the gospel of the Prince of Peace; and years afterward Saint Thomas found them in India, baptized them and ordained them priests. Later they were martyred, and the Empress Helena is said to have found their bones and enshrined them in the Cathedral of Saint Sophia in Constantinople. During the crusades these relics were taken to Milan and later to Cologne where today they are to be found in the cathedral of that city in a chest of gold incrusted with jewels.

The article of food which comes first to mind for this feast is the famous Twelfth Day cake, baked and eaten in many lands. In France the *Galette des Rois* is cut carefully so that there will be one more piece than there are guests at the table. This, called *la part de Dieu*, goes to the first poor person who comes to the door. In Greece this is a double feast day for it is also that of Saint Basil, and the first piece of cake is cut for Christ, the next for Our Lady, and the third for Saint Basil.

When the cake is not divided according to purely religious custom, it is often considered a cake of luck. A bean is hidden in the cake, among other fortunetelling trinkets, and whoever finds this is crowned king or queen of the feast. France, in fact, has a proverb which comes directly from this finding of the lucky bean: *Il a trouvé la fève au gâteau.*

On the eve of the feast in Austrian homes, a blessing is invoked on the house and on each room individually. One of the family, carrying a shovel filled with coals and incense, goes from room to room followed by all the rest. When every room has been blessed, the household marches to the barn to bless the home of the animals too. And on that night the Christmas tree is lighted for the last time.

At Drury Lane Theatre in London a custom prevailed called "cutting the Baddeley Cake." A comedian of that name left the provision in his will that on each Twelfth Night the performers at the theater be served cake and wine from the interest of a fund he bequeathed for that purpose. So each year the cake was cut with great ceremony on the stage. And it is also from England that we have the best recipe for a Twelfth Day Cake.

Twelfth Day Cake

- 1 cup butter
- ¾ cup sugar
- 3 eggs
- ¼ cup milk
- 3 cups flour
- ¾ cup currants
- ¾ cup sultanas
- 4 tablespoons citron
- 4 tablespoons orange peel
- 4 tablespoons shredded almonds
- 1 teaspoon cinnamon
- ¼ teaspoon allspice

Cream the butter with the sugar. Add the eggs one at a time and beat after each addition. Add the milk and beat all thoroughly. Mix a little of the flour with the various raisins and peels. Sift the flour with the spices and fold into the mixture. Finally add the fruits and almonds. Bake in a pan lined with waxed paper for two hours in a slow oven at 250° F. Formerly this cake was baked two or three months before it was to be used, then it was covered with almond paste and a thin white icing.

Traditionally Lamb's Wool was always served with Twelfth Day Cake.

Lamb's Wool

Add the pulp of 6 baked apples to 1 quart of strong hot ale, together with a small quantity of freshly ground nutmeg and some powdered ginger. Add granulated sugar to sweeten to taste. The mixture must be stirred "assiduously and let it be served hot."

JANUARY 15

Feast of Saint Paul the Hermit

Of the many men who during the early Christian centuries fled to live in the desert, Saint Paul the Hermit was the earliest. We have this on the testimony of none other than Saint Anthony who came there thinking that he himself was the first. Then, as *The Golden Legend* of Jacobus de Voragine tells the story, "he learned in a dream that another anchorite, better than himself, had a claim to this homage. Therefore, Saint Anthony bent every effort to discover the whereabouts of this other hermit. And searching through the forests, he came first upon a hippocentaurus, half man and half horse, who told him to go to the right. Next he met an animal who was carrying some dates; the upper part of his body was that of a man, but he had the belly and feet of a goat. Anthony asked him what he was; and he answered that he was a satyr, that is, one of those creatures which the pagans mistook for wood-gods. Finally Saint Anthony came face to face with a wolf, who led him to the cell where Saint Paul dwelt. But he, being aware of the approach of a man, had closed his door. Anthony besought him to open to him, declaring that he would die on the spot rather than go away. And Paul, yielding to his prayers, opened the door, and at once the two hermits embraced each other with great affection.

"When the noon-hour drew near, a crow flew down, bearing a loaf formed of two halves. Anthony wondered at this, but Paul told him that God provided him daily with food in this manner; this day the quantity was doubled, on account of Anthony's visit. Thereupon they disputed piously over which of them was more worthy to divide the loaf. Paul wished that Anthony should do it, since he was the guest. Anthony insisted that it be Paul, who was the older. In the end both took hold of the loaf, and broke it in two."

De Voragine does not go on to state the nature of the loaf, but we like to think of it as one of the simplest and best of whole wheat loaves.

Whole Wheat Bread

½ cake yeast	3 cups whole wheat flour
1 cup white flour	(No shortening, sugar, or milk)

Moisten the yeast with a little tepid water and allow it to stand for ten minutes. Add it to the flour and enough tepid water, together with a pinch of salt, to make a good dough. Let it stand until it doubles in bulk. Then punch it down, knead again, and put it into small bread pans. When it rises again to double its bulk, bake in a moderate oven at 350° F. for a full hour or more. Slice very thin.

JANUARY 21

Feast of Saint Agnes

Saint Agnes' day is the feast of a saint about whom there are many legends, although little is known historically save that she was very young and a martyr. On her feast day lambs are blessed in Rome, and from their wool is woven material for the pallia which the popes send to a new archbishop.

In some countries Saint Agnes is the saint of maidens, especially those who are looking for husbands. The eve of her feast is considered an auspicious time to find out who will be one's future mate, and there are several old-time ways said to achieve this. In England a girl took sprigs of thyme and of rosemary, sprinkled them three times with water, put one on each side of her bed, and then recited:

Saint Agnes, who's to lovers kind,
Come ease the trouble of my mind.

In her dreams then she saw the face of her future husband. Sometimes a maid ate instead a salt-filled egg from which the yolk had been removed. In that case her future husband came to her in her dreams and offered her water. In certain parts of England, young women made cakes of flour, salt, and water (surely a fasting rather than a feasting dish), which were called "dumb cakes" because without saying a word the young woman would go upstairs with one of these cakes—backwards, to make it harder—get into bed, eat her cake, and pray fervently to Saint Agnes. There seems to be no record of disappointments, and we trust that all of those to whom Saint Agnes showed the dream face of her future got her man. Nor is there any record of how these cakes were made.

FEBRUARY 1

Feast of Saint Bridget

February is the shortest of months, one with few feasts, and usually beginning the year's greatest fast, Lent. The name's origin is from *Februarius*, the Roman feast of purification, but it is still a fitting name for this most Christian season.

The first feast in February is that of Saint Bridget, known lovingly in her own land as "Mary of the Gael." According to the scholars the name is rightly Brigit, but the common spelling is Bridget, and hers is the name borne by more girls in Ireland than any save one, that of Mary. In many legends she is associated with Saint Patrick, who is said to have baptized her and who had her help in converting Ireland; when he died it was she who stitched his shroud. Born about 450, she founded the nunnery of Kildare, the first on Irish soil.

In Celtic lands the dandelion is called "Saint Brigit's flame," so every time you see this flower think of that bright flame of faith, Saint Bridget, who carried on the work of Saint Patrick and whose watchword was "mercy." In the hearts of the Irish, Bridget stands for all that is sweetest and best and most human in women. An old story tells that she was born of a slave mother and taken from her at birth, but when she was older she set out to rejoin the lonely old woman and found her "at a mountain dairy having twelve cows with her, and she collecting butter." This legend doubtless explains why Bridget is considered the protectress of dairy workers and also this verse of "The Prayer of Saint Brigit":

> *O my Prince of Heaven!*
> *Bless a prayer unbidden—O pure Whiteness*
> *Bless a kitchen that hath butter!*

It is told that "everything Bridget put her hand to increased and grew beautiful," and in old stories she is shown feeding her hungry hounds with the table meat and brewing ale for the churches. Baskets filled with apples and fragrant bread are "Brigit alms," and it is said she left to her countrywomen her gift of simple healing—for most Irish women have some elementary knowledge of medicine and herbal remedies.

Bridget is well known not only in Irish households but also in English, for she was a favorite saint in the Britain of an early day. In London an ancient well, named Saint Bride's Well in her honor, lent its name to the nearby Brideswell Palace which Edward VI turned into a workhouse for the poor in later years.

On her feast special cakes were served with ale, called *Barinbreac*, and sometimes *Barmbrack* or *Barnbreak*.

Barinbreac

- 4 oz. butter
- 1½ lbs. flour
- 2 teaspoons baking soda
- 2 tablespoons currants
- 1 tablespoon caraway seeds
- sugar
- buttermilk

Rub the butter into the flour which has been sifted with the soda. Add the currants and the caraway seeds and a very little sugar. Add sufficient buttermilk to make a wet dough—one that will drop into the pan. Bake at 300° F. for two hours.

Irish women are in general great makers of delectable cakes and breads for special occasions—of ash cakes (little scones rolled in cabbage leaves) baked in the ashes on the hearth and when done sopped in rasher gravy; of tea scones made with golden meal and baked on the griddle, delicious eaten with jelly or jam; of white bread and brown, Indian meal and bran loaves; of seedy cakes and Sunday cakes.

They were also adept at making the jellies and jams that fill the odd places on a well-set Irish table—sloe jelly, rowanberry jelly, haw-and-apple jelly, damson preserves and blackberry jam, to mention but a few. And since the daughters of Saint Bridget are great believers in natural remedies, they are apt to insist that the children eat

Parsley Jelly

Take 3 bunches of parsley and set to boil with sufficient water to cover. Boil for about twenty-five minutes and strain through a jelly bag. Return the strained liquid to the fire and simmer for an additional ten minutes. Measure your juice and allow 1 pound of sugar for each 2 cups of liquid, boil together until jelly sets or drops from the spoon. Peel 1 lemon thinly, tie in a bit of cheesecloth, and add during last ten minutes of cooking. Pour into hot, sterilized jars and cover with paraffin.

FEBRUARY 2

Candlemas Day or Feast of the Purification

The feast which falls on this day is known both as Candlemas and the feast of the Purification of the Blessed Virgin. It was begun in order to counteract the pagan observances of ancient Rome at that season, when the whole city was lighted with candles and torches in honor of the Roman goddess Februa. It was likewise the month dedicated to the gods of the underworld, and candles also represented Ceres who was trying to find her daughter Proserpina, stolen from her by Pluto and carried by him to the lower world.

At first a pagan religious celebration, it grew into an occasion of mere merrymaking and night-long revels, and at last Sergius, one of the early popes, changed the festival into a Christian feast in honor of the purification of the Virgin Mary.

On that day candles for the year are blessed in Christian churches and lighted ones carried in procession. It is very natural that long ago in England it received its name of Candle Mass. To Christians the candles are symbolic of Christ, the light of the world, and of Simeon's reference to the Child brought by Our Lady to the Temple as "a light to the revelation of the Gentiles." The candles blessed on this day are in many places given to the faithful, and carefully kept for use in time of need, as during childbirth and at the hour of death.

In England in olden times there was a belief that if Christmas greens were left up longer than this day, as many goblins would appear and trouble the house as there were leaves or branches remaining. One would think that all Christmas decorations would have been disposed of by this time, but perhaps sentimental souls left theirs hanging long beyond the classic day for taking them down—the day after Epiphany. One can sympathize, for it is much more pleasant to put up a symbol of joy than to remove it. No doubt this superstition was created to make such soft souls face duty and put down lingering regret.

In some parts of Mexico on this day godparents entertain a group of guests, and in other places the party is given by the guest who found the little replica of the Christ Child in his slice of the *Rosca de Reyes*, which is none other than our old friend the *Galette des Rois*, the Twelfth Day Cake.

FEBRUARY 3

Feast of Saint Blaise

Saint Blaise, who is invoked against diseases of the throat, was a bishop of an early century who was driven to the mountains by persecution and took refuge in a cave infested with wild beasts. But Saint Blaise so subdued them that each morning they came to him to ask his blessing. After a period of peace he was discovered, dragged before the prefect, and condemned to imprisonment and eventual death. But even while a captive he healed a child choking to death from a fishbone and made a wolf give back to a poor woman the pig it was stealing from her.

He is a much beloved saint and always willing to help those in trouble. In the Middle Ages it was a common thing to "call upon God and remember Saint Blaise."

On his feast day the heads of households among the Basques of the Pyrenees bring to the church garlic, salt, apples, and chocolates for Saint Blaise's blessing, and later give these to their children and their animals for protection against throat ailments. Of their own throats, the adults take less care, for the great Basque festival dish is *loukinkas*, a regional sausage highly seasoned with peppers. These sausages are served with fresh raw oysters, and the height of gastronomic delight is to eat a *loukinkas* and follow it with a cool fresh oyster to take away the burning sensation.

Pre-Lenten Festivals

Unless Easter is very late indeed, the beginning of Lent falls in February. Easter Sunday is the first Sunday after the full moon which occurs on or next after March 21st; it therefore always falls on some date between March 22nd and April 25th inclusive.

In various countries there are customs for these days

which have survived the centuries and are still lovingly observed. And nearly always there is some special dish that is prepared during this time.

In Poland high feasting takes place on the Thursday before Lent, and the day's specialty is *Piczki*, rich fried doughnuts. In Syria the Thursday before Lent is known as Drunkard's Thursday because eating and drinking reach top form on that day. A sheep is slaughtered and roasted and served with rice-stuffed grape leaves and figs stewed in molasses.

Dolmas (Stuffed Grape Leaves)

- grape leaves
- ½ cup rice
- ½ cup chick-peas
- 1 onion
- 2 cloves garlic
- 1 tablespoon parsley
- salt
- pepper

Blanch the grape leaves in boiling water for about five minutes. Combine the rice with the chick-peas (either canned or cooked), the minced onion, garlic, parsley, and seasoning. Place a tablespoon of this mixture on each leaf, roll up and press together with your hand. Cook them for about thirty minutes with enough water to cover, or some tomato juice seasoned liberally with lemon. They may be eaten hot or cold. If you have no grape leaves, cabbage leaves (remove the spine) or even lettuce leaves may be used.

On the Friday before Lent, in Ponti in Italy the people of the town celebrate the feast of *Polentone* when an enormous dish of *polenta*, weighing more than a thousand pounds, is prepared and with it an omelet said to contain six thousand eggs, put together by the best cooks in town. We should like to see with our own eyes an omelet of six thousands eggs being turned over, since turning one made of only six is quite a trick, but no doubt the cooks of Ponti have had experience. These huge dishes are given to the poor. Evidently the cooking is the thing in this case;

the eating is secondary to the wonder of constructing the dishes. This recipe makes a quantity considerably smaller than the wonder of Ponti but equally good.

Pasticcio di Polenta (Corn Meal Pie)

1 cup yellow corn meal
butter
bread crumbs
cream
Parmesan cheese
salt
handful dried mushrooms

In the morning of the day this dish is to be served, cook the corn meal in only enough water to make it very stiff. Turn out to cool in just the shape of the dish in which it was cooked. When preparing the *pasticcio,* butter the same dish in which the corn meal was cooked and sprinkle with bread crumbs. Cut the molded corn meal in horizontal strips about ¼ inch thick. Lay the top slice in the bottom of the dish where it fits. Dot with a little butter and 3 or 4 dried mushrooms which have had boiling water poured over them and have soaked for several hours. Moisten with cream and sprinkle with grated Parmesan. Repeat slice by slice until the shape is complete. Put in a moderate oven at 300° F. and bake for three hours.

In Paris, Carnival, as it is called, is limited to the three days preceding Ash Wednesday; on the last day there is a procession of the *Boeuf Gras* through the streets. In Switzerland during these days children receive cakes flavored with caraway seeds.

But it is in Denmark that children come into their own during this time. The Monday before Ash Wednesday is a holiday known as *Fastelaven.* While their parents are still in bed, the children of the family, armed with twigs called Lenten birches, come into their parents' rooms where the latter are supposedly asleep, but no doubt wide awake and ready to make sure their offspring do not become too violent with the instruments of punishment in their hands. "Give buns," shout the young, and the parents produce for them the *Fastenlavensboller.* We take if for granted that parents may then take one more bit of slumber, at least for the time it takes the children to consume their buns. They are toothsome morsels.

Fastenlavensboller (Lenten Buns)

1 yeast cake	½ teaspoon cardamon seeds
¾ cup sugar	¾ cup butter
1½ cups lukewarm milk	½ cup raisins
3¼ cups flour	

1 egg

Let the yeast stand with a little sugar in a little lukewarm milk. Sift the flour with the rest of the sugar and the ground cardamom seeds, and stir in the milk and butter which has been melted. Combine with the yeast mixture and raisins, and work until smooth. Let it stand and then knead, roll out fairly thick and cut out buns with a round cutter. Let rise again, brush with beaten egg, and bake in a moderate oven at 375° F. for half an hour.

Collop Monday

In England the Monday before Lent is known as Collop Monday, so called because it was the last day of eating meat before the fast began. In an earlier day fresh meat was cut into collops, or steaks, for salting or hanging until after Lent was over. It is still customary to have eggs and collops, or eggs and bacon on this day.

English Eggs and Bacon

Cut strips of bacon in 3-inch lengths, place them in a baking dish, and pour over them 3 tablespoons of cream. Bake in a moderate oven until the bacon is brown on one side, and then turn it over and brown the other. While the bacon is cooking, poach your eggs and serve on the bacon. This could be attractively done in individual ramekins.

Italians in many rural areas who celebrate a pre-Lenten *Carnevale* lasting for four weeks before Lent, begin on this Monday the last and gayest days of all. They are called "The Two Days of the Shepherds," and all work is suspended while feasting, dancing, and merrymaking take place in the public squares, ending with a masquerade on the night of Shrove Tuesday. Traditional during these two days of festivity is a dish called *Salsiccia con Peperoni* (sausage with green peppers).

Salsiccia con Peperoni (Sausage with Green Peppers)

Take 2 to 2½ pounds of Italian sausage and see to it that it remains in one piece. Curl in broiling pan and broil about 5 inches from flame for about half an hour. Sauté 4 green peppers and 1 sweet onion, both cut up, in a little olive oil and serve with the sausage which should be well browned by this time. Be sure to prick the sausage once or twice while it is cooking.

Shrove Tuesday

All other pre-Lenten celebrations pale when one comes to Shrove Tuesday. The name comes, of course, from the practice of confessing one's sins on that day, of being shriven in preparation for the season of penance to come. But in many parts of the world, especially in olden times, people had a great deal else on their minds on Shrove Tuesday, that is, a great deal on the subject of food. The cooks outdid themselves on special dishes, ignoring completely the fact that the way to come to a long fast would be to taper off, as is done with drugs.

In pre-Reformation times in English towns the church bell was rung on Shrove Tuesday and came to be known as the "shriving bell." This in time was called the "pancake bell," so closely identified was the day with that article of food.

Pancakes and fritters,
Say the bells of Saint Peter's,

runs the old rhyme about the bells of London. And in an almanac for 1684 we find:

Hark I hear the pancake bell
And fritters make a gallant smell.

But pancakes were by no means all they ate in Merrie England on Shrove Tuesday; they enjoyed hogs, barbecued whole, basted with wine, and stuffed with spicy meals. Yet pancakes were the day's specialty—pancakes of all kinds, thin like modern ones; or fat, rich fritters with fruit cut into them for flavor.

Later in England the Puritans looked upon such observances with a jaundiced eye, and an English cookery book of the seventeeth century describes pancakes as made with water, eggs, "spices and magical, tragical enchantments" and of "sweet bait which ignorant people devore very greedily." Even *Crêpes Suzettes* would hardly rate such harsh words. But it is clear that the Puritans regarded the pancakes as merely one more popish dish and so came out against it. One feature of the custom should have pleased their economical souls, since the pancakes used up all the fat in the household, as at that time none could be used for the next six weeks.

The French eat pancakes on Shrove Tuesday too; however, they make them folded, not flat as we do. To them a cold pancake is as good as a hot one, and with these cold pancakes they drink wine. However, *Crêpes Suzettes,* their most famous and sophisticated version, are not only served hot but flaming.

Today in England and the United States the pancake is traditional, and much attention is given to the feat of turning them deftly from side to side. In our country in earlier days, when the mother of the family fried the pancakes, she was watched critically to see how well she could "flap" them—the origin of the word flapjack.

Buttermilk Pancakes

4 cups flour
½ teaspoon baking soda
1 tablespoon sugar
pinch of salt
½ teaspoon cream of tartar
4 tablespoons butter
buttermilk

Sift the dry ingredients and rub in the butter. Add just enough buttermilk so that the batter pours easily, like heavy cream. An egg may be added if desired. Bake on a lightly greased griddle.

The Irish Boxty Pancakes are always made with buttermilk, and are eaten hot with butter and sugar as fast as they come from the pan. They are made of grated raw potato, flour, salt, soda, buttermilk, and eggs. And into the ingredients are dropped little charms, wrapped in paper: a ring for the one first to be married, a thimble for an old maid, a button for a bachelor, a cross for the one who would enter religion, and a sixpence for riches. These pancakes are usually served at tea time with a black brew of Irish tea.

Some lands scorn the pancake, and in Scotland, perhaps just to be different, people eat Crowdy on Shrove Tuesday. A description of this dish sounds much like the usual fare of the Scots, for it is made by pouring boiling water over oatmeal and stirring it a little. Perhaps the butter and milk that went over it is not for every day. And there is another variation: into the porringer of one unmarried person in the house is put a ring, and whoever finds this in his or her bowl will be the first to be married.

In Germany *Fastnachtskuchen,* doughnuts and not pancakes, are eaten on the eve of the Lenten fast, and the Pennsylvania Germans in the United States follow this same custom. Here is their recipe:

Fastnachtskuchen (Shrove Tuesday Doughnuts)

2 cups milk	1 cup sugar
1 cake yeast	3 eggs
½ cup water	¼ cup lard
6 cups flour	1 teaspoon salt

Scald the milk and allow to cool. Dissolve the yeast in the water which should be warm and add ½ cup of flour, sifted. Mix thoroughly. Add this to the milk with a little of the sugar. Then add 3 cups of flour, sifted, and let rise, preferably overnight. Beat the eggs well and add with the lard and the rest of the sugar. Mix well. Stir in enough of the remaining flour to make a stiff dough. Let it rise again. Turn out on a floured pastry board and roll to ¼-inch thickness. Cut out and let the doughnuts rise to double their bulk. Fry in deep fat at 360° F. for three to four minutes, turning as they fry. Drain on absorbent paper.

The Swedes make a rich yeast bun for Shrove Tuesday. After baking, the top of the bun is cut off, the inside scooped out, and the hollow filled with almond paste. The buns are put in soup plates and eaten with hot milk flavored with almonds and vanilla sugar. These have become so popular that Swedish folk serve them every Tuesday all through Lent. These buns are known as *Fet Tisdags Bullar*.

Filling for *Fet Tisdags Bullar* (Fat Tuesday Buns)

1 cup blanched almonds	¾ cup sugar
	heavy cream

Scoop out about two tablespoons from one bun after the top has been cut off and mix with blanched almonds, which have been finely chopped or ground, and the sugar, preferably confectionery sugar. Add sufficient heavy cream to make a soft paste. To flavor the hot milk which is poured over these buns, steep a two-inch piece of vanilla bean in the milk for ten minutes. (Usually a few bitter almonds are included in the paste.)

In the Netherlands is eaten the *Worstebrod* that looks like a plain loaf of bread, but the inside is filled with sausage meat, the last eaten before Lent. In Belgium *Waterzoei*, essentially a Flemish dish, is popular on this day as well as throughout Lent. The recipe is flexible and can be adapted to one's personal taste.

Waterzoei (Fish Soup)

2 lbs. fish	white pepper
3 tablespoons butter	salt
1 carrot	wine and water
1 onion	1 lemon
3 cloves	sprig of parsley

thyme

The fish used in *Waterzoei* (it is called *Waterzootje* in Dutch) is traditionally carp, eel, tench, roach, perch, or barbel but any combination may be used. Cut off the heads and tails of your fish and fry them lightly in butter, adding the minced carrot and onion, the herbs and the spices. Add ⅓ water and ⅔ dry white wine to generously cover. Let this bouillon simmer for half an hour, then add your fish, cut in 2-inch lengths, and cook quickly for another twenty minutes or until the fish is done. Just before serving add a peeled lemon, cut into thin slices and with the seeds removed. The soup is served with thin slices of brown bread spread with butter. Our informant adds, "For some tastes, the heads and tails should be removed before serving the dish"—with which we would agree heartily.

In the southern part of the United States, Mardi Gras —Fat Tuesday—has long been extravagantly celebrated. Many of the inhabitants of New Orleans particularly are of French descent, so it is not strange that the Shrove Tuesday festivities of Paris were brought to the New World, and even improved upon. In New Orleans these end a gay season of parades and balls, very costly in general, and organized by groups known as *krewes*. The king of the whole Carnival is chosen by the Rex *krewe* and takes a leading role in the parade and in the revelries and feasting that follow. Private and public dinners are given before the grand ball on the evening of Mardi Gras, and among other items of excellent creole cookery is certain to appear

Crème Brulée Créole

8 eggs
2 cups light cream
brown sugar
2 tablespoons white granulated sugar
pinch of salt

Beat your eggs well into the cream, adding the granulated sugar and salt. Cook slowly in a double boiler, stirring constantly until as thick as custard. Pour into a baking dish and set aside to cool. When the custard has set, cover with 1 inch of brown sugar. Place under a preheated broiler for about five minutes, taking care that the sugar does not burn. When cold, place in refrigerator until ready to use.

Ash Wednesday

We have finished with the feastings of Shrove Tuesday now, and they are a memory only, a haunting aroma, a vanished delight. We have come to Ash Wednesday, *dies cinerum*, the beginning of Lent.

The origin of the Lenten fast, historically considered, is very obscure. It may have evolved from an ancient one-day fast, which preceded every Sunday, into the forty-day fast which precedes the greatest feast of the Christian year. But this fast is very old in time and dates back almost to Apostolic days. The number forty has many analogies—the number of days of the fast of Elias, of the years of the wandering of the Israelites; of the days of the Flood, of Moses on Mount Sinai, and of Christ in the desert. Saint Irenaeus mentions variations of its length—a day, forty hours, several days. The one day which was always kept as a fast day is that of Good Friday.

In early times, as now, food eaten during Lent was a matter of deep interest—what to eat and what not to eat. One historian of the fifth century says that "some abstain from every creature that has life, but that others eat fish; that some eat also birds because in the account of the creation these too sprang from the water. And some eat no fruit with a hard shell and some eat no eggs, and some eat dry bread only and others hardly that."

We have fasters of that intense sort today too. There is a super-observance and an under-observance, depending on the person. We know a woman who carefully weighs the amount of bread she eats during Lent so that she does not eat a crumb too much. She has the right idea no doubt because your eyes might give you another piece but your scales won't!

None of us, of course, fast today as they did in long-ago centuries, when eggs and butter were taboo and when often the standard diet for Lent consisted only of bread, salt, and water. We doubt whether we could get through a day on bread only, and this is strange, for the people of other days were really better trenchermen than we. Any ancient cookery book will prove that. Why is it then that the modern quails at a diet of bread when this was the sole food taken on any fast day in medieval times?

The writer of a recent article, Julie Bedier, gives one explanation. She says, in an article in *The Commonweal*, it is because in those days bread was always bread. She writes of the bread of the peasant, a meal in itself, dark brown and solid and substantial, as compared with the urban white bread that is "like a nice, tender paper towel." She feels it would be quite easy to keep a fast on such bread, a complete meal with vitamins intact for desk workers and laborers alike. She may be right at that.

We would add one other food item to hers—a good big salad at least once a day. And, of course, plenty of hot coffee. If those three foods make a fast, we are for it. The only problem that remains is how to get simple peasant bread out of a modern bakery.

One thing, however, is certain, and that is that fish is a standard food for Lent. The range of choice is certainly wide here, with simple recipes for simple folk and complicated recipes for complicated people. A cookery book of over a hundred years ago mentions two varieties for different castes: for the ordinary you and me there is suggested salt fish with parsley and egg sauce; for the epicure, a dish of turbot with wine gravy and capers.

Egg and Parsley Sauce

2 hard-boiled eggs
1 tablespoon parsley
white sauce
lemon juice
onion juice

Chop the eggs coarsely and mix with the finely minced parsley. Add this to your white (or cream) sauce which has been flavored with lemon and onion juice.

In our democratic way, we can range from a plain slice of codfish to lobster thermidor. An unusual sauce hailing from the Mediterranean is *Aïoli*, which is really mayonnaise made with garlic, and at times, with bread crumbs. It is served with many things but usually with boiled fish.

Aïoli

3 cloves garlic
2 egg yolks
pepper
salt
mustard
1⅓ cups olive oil
lemon juice

Start by pounding 3 cloves of garlic and then add the egg yolks, seasonings, and then the oil, drop by drop, just as you would in making mayonnaise. A few drops of lemon juice are added at the end.

There is still another group of persons who do not like fish in any form, and to them fish is just fish no matter how regal its birth or how great a chef prepares it. These folk might ponder on Saint Corentinus, patron saint of Quimper, a hermit of the sixth century. He lived in a forest, close to a stream; each morning a fish, sent by the angels to nourish him, swam to the bank where he lived. Corentinus cut a slice off of it for his daily meal. Then the fish swam away, evidently feeling happy about the whole thing. Next day he returned promptly to be again amputated.

The Irish have a good substantial dish for Lent which is fishless. With them Champ is a favorite dinner for the Lenten season. It is composed of freshly boiled, peeled potatoes, drained and then pounded with a beetle (Irish for potato masher). While the potatoes are being pounded, a vegetable such as nettles, or scallions, or perhaps parsley or chives, which have been boiled in milk, is added. Each person is given a large plateful, a hole is made in the center, and into this a large lump of butter is put. Champ is eaten from the outside with a fork or spoon, dipping it into the melting butter in the center. The whole is washed down with freshly churned buttermilk.

Ash Wednesday is observed as a day of absolute fast in many parts of the world. It is not in any case a day for varied menus, but rather one for church attendance and dietetic simplicities. In Spain on this day a strip of pork is cut in the shape of a fish and buried with pomp and ceremony, to signify that there will be less meat on the table for some time to come, and this is called the *entierro de la sardina.*

England had a pudding for this day—Stir-up Pudding. It was considered wrong to spend time cooking on Ash Wednesday, and this pudding was one which could be stirred up in a hurry, for it consisted only of milk and flour and fruit syrups. Later it was called Hasty Pudding and so the English call it today.

Austrians make a pretzel for this day called *Fasten-*

brezel. This is very appropriate, for the pretzel had a religious origin. In other centuries these were made in monasteries and were shaped like a ring with a cross above them. They were known by the Latin name *pretiolum,* which means a little prize. The monks, so the story goes, gave them as prizes to good students and sometimes to all in their schools who had been good children. From this Latin word has evolved our plebian word pretzel, and of course it is easy to see from its shape that it might well have started in life as a circle and a cross.

FEBRUARY 14

Feast of Saint Valentine

During this month, sometimes within Lent and sometimes before it begins, comes a festival that is everyone's day—Saint Valentine's. It is the day of lovers' meetings and lovers' greetings. Whether the custom still exists, we don't know, but in our school days we had a box into which everyone put "valentines" for those toward whom he felt a tender passion or even a small affection. It led to unhappy results, for when the box was opened and the children's names were called, the flip little party with golden curls and vacuous blue eyes had her desk piled high, while the good little girl, who cleaned the blackboards after school, had uninteresting braids, and wore glasses, got only one or possibly two.

Life, it is true, may be just like that, but perhaps more than one female of uncertain age is telling her psychoanalyst about one of those valentine boxes.

At all events, Valentine's Day is a day of love. In the Middle Ages there was a belief that on this day the birds began to mate, and Chaucer speaks of

Seynt Valentyne's Day,
When every foul cometh to choos hys mate.

The identity of the saint who started all this is really not known. There were three Valentines, all saints and martyrs, and all honored on this day. One died in Rome, one was a bishop at Terni, and one came from Africa. It is the bishop who is usually associated with the celebration of this day. Certainly, whoever he may be, he has made it a pleasant feast, and Charles Lamb calls him "the great immortal go-between."

In Leicestershire, England, lozenge-shaped buns, made with caraway seeds and currants, called Valentine Buns were formerly given to old people and children. The old-fashioned Valentine cookies, cut into heart shapes, sprinkled with red sugar, and decorated with red and white frosting, or even gilt, have also gone out of style. They should be revived.

Saint Valentine Cookies

2½ cups brown sugar	1 tablespoon ginger
1½ cups cream	½ grated lemon rind
1 cup molasses	8 cups flour

3 teaspoons soda

Beat the sugar into the cream until it is thickened but not stiff; then add the molasses, ginger, and lemon rind and mix thoroughly. Sift the flour with the soda and add this to the first mixture. Knead until smooth and chill several hours, or better still, overnight. Roll out dough ⅛ inch thick, cut into desired shapes (hearts of course!) and bake at 275° F. for fifteen minutes. Allow to cool before removing from sheet. Decorate!

MARCH 1

Feast of Saint David

The first day of March marks the day of a saint who would seem to have no association with the culinary art but who is known to have had the leek as his symbol. The figure of David, the principal patron of Wales, is shrouded in legend, but he is said to have been a monk and a bishop; he is popularly supposed to have been a nephew of King Arthur.

It is told that when his people were engaged in a bitter battle against the Saxons, both armies looked alike in battle dress, and so close was the fighting that it was very hard to distinguish between friend and foe. David suggested that the Welsh soldiers wear a leek in their hats so that they could be readily identified from the enemy. They obeyed and won the battle. Thereafter the leek became the national symbol of Wales, and it is still worn by Welshmen on this day. The wearing and eating of the leek is a way of designating the true Taffy even away from home, and at Jesus College, Oxford, much frequented by Welshmen, Saint David's Day is marked by the undergraduates wearing real leeks; and a dinner is given, attended by the Fellows, who wear artificial ones in their buttonholes.

There is an excellent soup which has this vegetable as its chief ingredient.

Welsh Leek Soup

4 large leeks
4 potatoes
6 cups water
salt
1 onion
butter
2 egg yolks
½ cup cream
pepper

Carefully wash the leeks and cut them into narrow strips. Peel the potatoes, slice them, and cook them in the water with a pinch of salt until soft. Mince an onion, mix with the leeks, and sauté in a little butter till soft but not brown. Add to the potatoes. When the vegetables are quite soft, put them through a fine sieve and return to the liquid. Beat 2 egg yolks and mix with the cream; put in a tureen and add a little of the hot soup, stirring all the while. Season to taste. Add the rest of the soup and serve.

MARCH 17

Feast of Saint Patrick

The great Irish Patrick follows the Welsh David in our roll call of the saints. His name means the patrician, and he was the son of highborn Roman parents who were Christians, his father holding the office of *decurio* in Gaul or Britain. Captured by Irish marauders when he was a lad, he was taken to Ireland and sold into slavery; after six years he escaped and returned to his native land. But he had grown to love the Ireland of his captivity, and he set his heart on its conversion to Christianity. Serenely he went ahead with his mission and prepared himself under the guidance of a relative, Saint Martin of Tours, at the island monastery of Lérins. Arriving in Ireland to begin his work, Patrick was bitterly opposed by the Druids, but he preached and taught there for many years and succeeded in establishing the Christian faith.

His feast is one of high celebration not only in the Ireland of his love and labors but in the United States as well. In fact, one admiring Irish visitor, seeing the celebrations of this day in New York City, gave the highest praise he could when he remarked that they "excelled those in Dublin itself."

And no doubt he had little difficulty in finding in New York the potato dish he would have eaten on that day in his own Dublin. This, called Colcannon, is one of Ireland's favorites, since for the Irish "a day without potatoes is a day without nourishment"; and he would have doubtless covered it with a rich brown gravy of some kind.

Colcannon

1 lb. cold boiled potatoes	4 tablespoons bacon fat
1 onion	2 cups boiled cabbage

salt and pepper

Mash the potatoes. Mince the onion and fry lightly in the bacon fat (butter may be substituted). Mix potatoes, cabbage which has been chopped, and the onion and season with salt and pepper. Grease a baking dish, pour in the mixture, and bake for thirty minutes in a moderate oven at 350° F.

And he would certainly try to find:

Irish Soda Bread

2 lbs. flour	1 teaspoon baking soda
1 teaspoon salt	1 cup buttermilk

1 teaspoon cream of tartar

Sift the flour and the dry ingredients into a bowl. Make a hole in the center and stir in the buttermilk. If too dry, add a little more milk. Make a rather stiff dough, divide into 2 loaves, and bake on a greased pan in a moderate oven at 350° F. for forty-five minutes.

Back in his own country our Irishman would have eaten (for all fast-day laws are suspended on Saint Patrick's Day) succulent chops, boiled ham, roast chicken, or good roast beef, and these he could easily find in New York too.

But he would have had trouble locating an Irish extra-special dish such as this eaten only on great occasions:

Jellied Pig's Head

Clean the pig's head thoroughly, split it in two, and allow it to pickle for four days in a brine made of one part salt to nine parts water. Then put into a large pot, cover with water, and add 1 large onion quartered, a clove of garlic (optional), the rind of 1 lemon, 1 bay leaf, 6 whole peppercorns, and 6 whole cloves. Bring to a boil and then allow to simmer for three to four hours, that is, until the meat is tender but unbroken. The most delicate part of the next operation is removing all of the bones while still retaining the shape of the head. The tongue may be cut up and inserted in various places where the cooking has caused a loss of fat. Place the head in a deep bowl and cover with the stock, adding salt if necessary and a little white vinegar, just enough to make it tart. Set in a cool place until the stock has jellied. Unmould and cut in very thin slices. Serve with a necklace of parsley.

MARCH 19

Feast of Saint Joseph

Two days after the feast of the great Irish saint comes the day of the carpenter of Nazareth, Saint Joseph, "the just man," of whom the Gospels say little but whom the world has taken to its heart. Although he is often pictured as an aged man, bearded and bent with years, we incline to the concept of a younger Joseph, more fitted to his role as protector of the young Mary and her Child.

Saint Joseph is patron of many places and many trades. He is the patron of the spiritual home of Christians, the Church, and of their material homes as well.

Generosity marks this day, as it did the character of Joseph himself. In many nations it is a day of sharing with the poor and needy, and nowhere is this better carried out than in the nation which perhaps loves San Giuseppe the most—Italy. In many Italian villages, and especially in Sicily, everyone of any means contributes to a table spread in the public square as a thank offering for favors received from prayers to this kindly saint. The bread made for this day is often shaped like a scepter or a beard; villagers representing Jesus, Mary, and Joseph are guests of honor at the feast, and other guests are the orphans and widows and beggars. After Mass all go in procession to this festive table and, after the priest blesses the feast, everyone falls to with shouts of "*Viva la tavila di San Giuseppe!*" At the end of the meal every guest is given something to take home. At these feasts a good soup is usually served, preferably *Minestrone.*

Minestrone

½ lb. salt pork	2 tablespoons butter
2 qts. water	1 cup dried beans (soaked overnight)
1 clove garlic	salt and pepper
2 sprigs parsley	rice
2 carrots	½ cup peas
2 stalks celery	

½ small head of cabbage

Cut the rind from the pork and set it to boil in cold water. Cut off a small piece of the pork and pound it in a mortar, with the garlic and the parsley. Slice the carrots, the celery, the cabbage leaves (remove ribs), and add with the butter, the dried beans, salt and pepper to the boiling water. Then add the rest of the pork and allow to simmer for two and one-half hours. Then add a handful of rice for each person to be served together with the peas. Cook until rice is done.

Although all kinds of lentils and dried beans are eaten on Saint Joseph's feast, the cheese, usually so popular a part of the Italian diet, is not served, and instead of the usual grated Parmesan the *minestrone* would be served with dry toasted bread crumbs.

The traditional dessert is a cream puff known as *Sfinge di San Giuseppe.*

Sfinge (Sphinx Puffs)

1 cup pastry flour	1 tablespoon sugar
½ cup butter	4 eggs
1 cup water	grated orange peel
salt	grated lemon peel

Filling

1 lb. *ricotta* (Italian pot cheese)	2 tablespoons sugar
2 tablespoons chocolate	orange peel
	crème de cacao

To make your puffs, combine flour, butter, water, salt, and sugar in a saucepan and bring to a boil. Cook and stir until the mass leaves the side of the pan. Add eggs one at a time, beating well after each addition. Add a little grated orange and lemon peel. Drop by tablespoon on a baking sheet; bake at 400° F. for ten minutes and then reduce heat to 350° F. for another twenty-five minutes.

Stir until smooth the *ricotta,* chocolate, sugar, a little grated orange peel, and a generous dash of *crème de cacao* and use this to fill your puffs when they have cooled.

A special dessert made in Bologna for this feast is *Ravioli di San Giuseppe.* Made in the same way as other dumplings but with puff paste or short crust, they are filled either with marzipan or some kind of jam, and either baked in the oven or fried in oil to a rich golden color. In Naples *Zeppole* or cream fritters are traditional.

In Russia *Blini* are served with sour cream, and in Sweden a bun with cream and butter and bits of marzipan. Again in Italy little cakes filled with jam are hawked at street corners on Saint Joseph's Day. Sold right from the kettles in which they are cooked, they sometimes make the whole city smell like one vast bakeshop.

MARCH 21

Feast of Saint Benedict

We are told that when a youth of only fifteen years, Benedict fled from the gay life of Rome to the silence and solitude of a great forest. Young as he was, he knew exactly the life he wanted to lead, and it was that of a hermit. However, since he had not taken thought as to how to provide himself with food to sustain life, his childhood nurse insisted on following him and preparing for him the food she obtained by begging. Once when she broke a sieve which she had borrowed, Benedict by a miracle made it whole again.

But after some years of these ministrations, Benedict fled from her too, this time to a cave at Subiaco. There a hermit named Romanus brought him food for a while, but when Romanus died, there was no one to serve him. Then an angel took over and guided to the saint's cave a priest who carried with him a considerable store of provisions which he shared with the hermit of Subiaco.

Later, Benedict had to leave his beloved retreat for God needed him elsewhere, and at Monte Cassino, where had been altars to Venus and to Jupiter, he erected a great monastery and founded a great order and a rule of life described as "a monument of wisdom," and which has survived the centuries.

But in his early days Benedict was certainly the most waited-on saint in all the long list of hermits!

Since Saint Benedict's feast day falls in Lent, we suggest for his feast Eggs Benedict, although we are fully aware the saint did not invent this dish.

Lenten Eggs Benedict

Follow the usual procedure for Eggs Benedict using ½ toasted muffin and 1 poached egg for each portion. Before placing the egg on the muffin spread this generously with anchovy paste stirred with enough heavy cream so that it will spread easily. Then add your egg, cover with a good hollandaise, and place a thin slice of truffle or about 6 capers on top.

MARCH 25

Annunciation of the Blessed Virgin Mary

This feast celebrates the actual moment of the Incarnation, when the Angel Gabriel appeared to Mary in her home in Nazareth—a scene so often commemorated in art and story and marked by every ringing of the Angelus bell. In old calendars it is called Feast of the Incarnation, Beginning of the Redemption, Annunciation of Our Lord. It is now held as a feast in honor of Our Lady in the Western Church, although the Church of the East makes the day rather a feast of Christ.

This day, also known as Lady Day, has long been observed with high honor in many parts of the world. In Russia it was considered so solemn a feast that, according to popular tradition, "even the birds do not mate on this day." It is also the day of the years when, according to belief in the Tyrol, the swallows return from their winter sojourn. And they will tell you too that on September 8th, which is Mary's birthday, they will once again fly southward.

In Sweden this day is familiarly called *Vaffelsdagen* (Waffle Day), and here is a favorite recipe.

Swedish Waffles

1⅓ cups flour
½ teaspoon salt
2 cups sour cream
3 tablespoons water
½ cup butter

Sift the flour with the salt and add to the cream together with the water which should be ice cold. Keep this batter in the refrigerator for one to two hours. Then melt the

butter and add to the batter. Heat the waffle iron and bake your waffles as usual. Serve with lemon juice, sugar and cinnamon, or stewed lingonberries.

MID-LENT

Laetare or Mothering Sunday

Mid-Lent is marked by Laetare Sunday, a name given the day because this word, meaning rejoice, is the beginning of the Introit of the Mass. It is a break in the long weeks of Lent with their dark liturgical vestments and flowerless altars; on this day the vestments are rose in color and the altar is decked with blossoms.

It is called Rose Sunday too, because it is the day on which in Rome the Pope blesses the Golden Rose, an ornament made of gold and precious gems, with a receptacle within the blossom into which is poured balsam and powdered musk. The Pontiff prays that the Church may so bring forth the fruit of good works and "the perfume of the ointment of the Flower sprung from the root of Jesse." These Golden Roses are given from time to time to churches or cities or to persons who have been of great service to the Church.

This day is also known as Mothering Sunday, either from a reference in the Epistle read on the fourth Sunday of Lent or because of the former custom of visiting the cathedral, that is, the mother church, on that day. And there grew up, especially in England, the idea of visiting one's own mother and taking her a gift, a custom which has grown to very secular heights today in our country on Mother's Day. It began with the praiseworthy idea of wearing a flower in honor of one's mother and, though the practice is still followed, the simple posy has grown into expensive purchases of flowers and gifts of other kinds. Perhaps it would be better to forget this new notion and go back to the old custom of visiting the church, since by honoring Mother Church one honors all mothers. And a single flower and a prayer is surely better than a fine bouquet and no prayer.

Braggot was a favorite drink for this feast day, and the word comes from the Welsh words for malt and honey. Braggot was made by boiling a variety of spices in ale, and often honey was added. Though originally a Welsh drink, it became popular in many countries and was quaffed everywhere until tea replaced it.

One delicacy especially associated with Mothering Sunday is the Simnel Cake, a yeast cake very yellow in color because of the saffron and candied peel it contained. The simnels were wrapped in cloth and boiled, then brushed with egg and baked, making a very hard cake indeed, and giving rise to the story of the lady who used one for years as a footstool.

The name simnel seems to be derived from the Latin word for very fine flour, *simila*. Long before the above boiled and baked cake came into being, there was made an unleavened wafer of the same name. In those days the recipe was apparently very simple, calling only for fine wheat flour, for honey and anise to sweeten and flavor, and cold water to make a thin batter which was stamped with a wafering iron.

The later simnel cakes were much more complicated of structure, but they remained very popular despite the complaints of the bakers that too much hard work was involved in making them.

Candy, spice, eggs must take—
Chop and pound till arms do ache.

So runs one old rhymed recipe for simnels. And Herrick says of these cakes:

I'll to thee a simnel bring
'Gainst thou go a-mothering;
So that, when she blesses thee,
Half that blessing thou'lt give me.

There is a modern version of this cake which is quite good and worth the effort.

Simnel Cake

¾ cup butter
2 cups sugar
4 eggs
2 cups flour
⅓ cup shredded lemon and orange peel
1 cup currants
almond paste
½ teaspoon salt

Cream the butter and sugar till smooth. Add the eggs one at a time, beating after each addition. Sift the flour and salt, and add to the first mixture. Dust the peel and the currants with a little flour and add to the batter. Line a round cake tin with wax paper and pour in half of the dough. Add a layer of almond paste, then the remaining dough. Bake at 300° F. for one hour. Ice with a thin white icing flavored with a few drops of almond extract.

Passion Sunday, also called Carling Sunday

This Sunday marks the beginning of Passiontide, the two weeks between this day and Easter especially commemorating the Passion or sufferings of Christ, the time when pictures and statues in churches are veiled in purple.

There is no food connected with the idea of the Passion, but there is with an event said to have taken place on this Sunday and which gave the day its second title of Carling Sunday. According to the story, a famine in Newcastle, England, was relieved when on that day there came into the harbor a ship with a cargo of peas commonly known as carlings. Some authorities hazard the guess that the name came from a penitential Lenten practice of wearing hard peas within the shoe—certainly a most uncomfortable custom.

The peas from which the day takes its secondary title are a variety of gray or brown pea prepared sometimes as a soup, sometimes fried in butter after being steeped in water all night—"until they be tender got." To modern palates the soup would no doubt be far more palatable.

Pea Soup

1 cup split peas	2 diced carrots
1 stalk celery	1 sliced onion
6 peppercorns	1 bay leaf
8 cups water	salt

½ cup cream

Wash and soak the peas overnight or use the quick-cooking variety. Place with the remaining ingredients except the cream, to boil, or rather simmer for about two hours. Mash through a fine sieve and add more water if necessary. Mix a little flour with the cream and stir slowly into the soup. Serve with buttered croutons.

Another dish served in some countries on this Sunday was Frumenty, a very ancient dish indeed. It consisted of wheaten meal boiled in water and sweetened with sugar. There is a legend that this is the food with which Joseph regaled his brethren and that he gave a double portion to the one brother who had been kind to him, the young Benjamin.

Palm Sunday

This day in observance of Christ's triumphant entry into Jerusalem is everywhere commemorated. In Rome at the Basilica of Saint John Lateran, "the mother and head of all the churches in the city and in the world," are blessed branches of palm and olive trees, and in churches of every country palms or green branches of some kind are blessed and distributed to the congregation. These palms are saved carefully, later to be burned to ashes for the next year's ceremonies of Ash Wednesday.

Palm Sunday was sometimes called Hosanna Sunday

in past years, and was also known as the Flowery Festival because blossoms were intertwined with the palms. One of our American States owes its name to this custom: Florida was discovered on Palm Sunday of 1512, and the Spanish therefore named the day *Pascua Florida.*

In Sicily dust from the church floor is swept up on this day and spread over the fields, and in Russia boughs of pussy willow are blessed and waved over the grain as protection against the elements. In other countries very elaborately decorated "palms" are constructed by young men and their lasses. All week long they collect flowers, fruit, honeycombs, and other edibles, which are hung on a large cross and what is left over is fastened to a pole. Of course the most heavily laden of these prove most popular the couple who constructed them.

In the Tyrol it is the children who make elaborate "palms" woven with ribbons and decorated with apples, candy, and flowers. The structure is topped by a bunch of pussy willows, and these are called "palm kittens" by the Tyrolese. After the palms have been proudly displayed in the church and through the village, the creators of the fine affairs take them home and eat all that is edible.

In various parts of England this day is sometimes called Fig Sunday. Rich and poor eat figs on this day, and the markets of years ago were filled with this fruit on the eve of the feast. A rather odd item of the 1860's describing this custom says that "even the charity children are in some places regaled with them."

Why the custom of eating figs on this day came into being no one knows for certain, but some authorities suggest it may be from the tradition that Christ ate figs after His entry into Jerusalem. This is connected with the withering of the barren fig tree, related shortly after the account of the triumphant entry into Jerusalem in Saint Matthew's Gospel.

Fig Pudding

- ½ cup sugar
- ⅓ cup butter
- 2 cups bread crumbs
- 1 cup milk
- 4 eggs
- ¼ cup flour
- ½ teaspoon salt
- 1 teaspoon baking powder
- cinnamon
- nutmeg
- cloves
- ½ cup figs
- 1 cup seeded raisins

Cream the sugar and butter, add the bread crumbs and milk, and mix thoroughly. Add the beaten eggs, the flour sifted with salt and baking powder and a pinch of each of the spices, the figs which have been chopped, and the raisins. Fill a greased pudding mold three-quarters full, cover tightly, and steam for three hours. Serve with hard or lemon sauce.

Maundy Thursday

Maundy or Holy Thursday is of course the day commemorating the Last Supper and the institution of the Eucharist. The derivation of the word "maundy" has been given as the Saxon word *maund*, for the hamper originally used to hold provisions to be given to the poor, for it was a day of almsgiving and generosity to those in need. The word is also said to come from the old French word *maundier*, to beg. Most likely of its explanations is that it was named from the antiphon of the ceremony of the Washing of the Feet which takes place on that day: *Mandatum novum do vobis*—"A new commandment I give to you," words spoken by Our Lord to His disciples on the eve of His death.

A custom was prevalent in certain European countries that greens should be eaten on this day, coming no doubt from the Charoseth or Jewish meal of bitter herbs, and the day is sometimes called Green Thursday. Among the Pennsylvania Dutch, spinach and dandelion greens are still eaten on Holy Thursday to prevent spring illness, an idea no doubt brought from Germany where it is an ancient belief. Perhaps this was considered a tonic after the Lenten foods, vitamins for a system which for some weeks had been underfed and might be open to attack by some germ or virus. Since the idea seems a good one, we offer a spinach dish for this day.

Holy Thursday Spinach

Prepare your spinach in the usual manner. Chop it finely —do *not* put it through a grinder. Mince an onion, fry it lightly in 2 tablespoons of butter, dust with a little flour, and stir into your chopped spinach. Then add 1 cup of sour cream, stirring thoroughly. Boil 2 eggs until hard, slice, and place over your spinach in the shape of a cross.

In Czechoslovakia children are given for breakfast on Maundy Thursday what are called Judases, rather gruesome cakes shaped like a rope in commemoration of the tragic end of the betrayer. In Picardy the children who chant the hours of the services are rewarded with eggs.

In Macedonia little cakes are made called Turtledoves in the form of a bird and having cloves for eyes. Another custom followed there on Holy Thursday is the coloring of the eggs for Easter. The mother of the family, after decorating the first Easter egg and making with it the sign of the cross over her children, places it close to the icon of the *Panagia*—the Greek word for The All Holy, the common Greek name for Our Lady, a contraction of her full title: All Holy Mother of God.

Good Friday

In the Eastern Church this day is known as Great or Holy Friday. The Western title is supposed to be a corruption of the phrase "God's Friday," the day on which Christ died. On this day the bells are silenced, and in

France the children are told that they have flown to Rome to return only on Holy Saturday. In Italy on Good Friday children are even warned not to laugh when playing, because of the solemnity of the time.

In certain places this day is observed by so strict a fast that it is often called the Black Fast, because many do not eat at all until sundown. However, one article of food is intimately associated with and eaten on this day, and that is the Hot Cross Bun.

Hot Cross Buns originated in England, and more than one nursery rhyme and ballad contain references to them. Saffron plays a part in the better-class English Hot Cross Bun, but as a rule they are small and plain, well browned and with icing on top in the form of a cross.

Hot Cross Buns

1 yeast cake
¼ cup lukewarm water
1 cup milk
½ cup sugar
½ cup shortening
1 egg
¼ cup shredded citron
¼ cup seedless raisins
3 cups flour
½ teaspoon salt

Soften the yeast in the lukewarm water. Scald milk, add sugar and shortening, and cool. Add the beaten egg, the yeast, citron, raisins, and the flour sifted with the salt. Knead and let rise to double its bulk. Shape into buns, place on greased baking sheet, and let rise until light. Brush with a little milk and bake at 375°F. for about twenty minutes. When done, cover with powdered sugar in the shape of a cross or do the same with a thin icing.

There were many superstitions concerning this bun. In some families one was put aside and kept during the following year. If someone fell ill, a little of the bun was grated into water and given to the sick person to aid his recovery. And so much has this bread become a symbol of friendship that if two people break a bun between them and eat it, the English tradition runs:

Half for you and half for me,
Between us two shall goodwill be.

Perhaps if the warring nations, the ones for whom Good Friday was once a holy day observed by the Truce of God, and the ones to whom it still represents a basic fact in the life of the spirit, could be persuaded to break a Good Friday bun instead of each other's heads, the world might again progress in amity and friendship. They might all know Him again in the breaking of bread.

In many parts of Germany it is customary to eat only *Spätzle* and stewed fruits for the evening meal on Good Friday.

Spätzle (Dumplings)

- 1½ cups flour
- pinch of salt
- 2 eggs
- ½ cup milk
- ½ cup water
- bread crumbs
- ¼ lb. butter

Sift the flour with the salt into a bowl. Add the eggs and the milk and water. Stir until smooth. Then, with a fork dipped in boiling water, cut the dough in small pieces into boiling water. Boil for a few minutes until they rise to the top. Cover with bread crumbs fried in butter. Serve with warm stewed prunes or other dried fruits.

APRIL 1

Feast of Saint Hugh of Grenoble

April is the "opening month," the month of expectation of spring and new hope. Centuries ago April was considered the year's actual beginning, and in some ways this seems more fitting than our present arrangement. For the earth that has been hard and cold with winter is growing soft again with rain and sun, and in garden and woodland the early flowers are in bloom; the great resurgent mystery which we accept as commonplace is again before us. Even though Easter sometimes comes earlier, this month is, in truth, the month of the Resurrection and Risen Love.

There is a saint for this day, Hugh of Grenoble, who lived in the twelfth century and who sometimes left his bishopric to live for a time in a Carthusian monastery as a simple monk. Once, on arriving, he found the monks assembled in the refectory but with nothing to eat. He was told that some benefactor had indeed given them fowl but their rule forbade the eating of meat. When Saint Hugh saw their predicament, he promptly made the sign of the cross and changed the fowl into turtles.

Could there be anything more appropriate for this day, then, than Mock Turtle Soup?

Mock Turtle Soup

1 calf's head
butter
2 veal bones
1 lb. beef
6 onions
2 shallots
rind of 1 lemon
pinch of cayenne pepper
6 cloves
pinch of mace
pinch of basil
½ glass sherry
juice of 2 lemons

Plunge the calf's head into boiling water, let it remain for one minute, then remove and rub with a coarse towel. Bone the head, put it into a saucepan, cover with cold water, and skim several times as it boils. Butter the bottom of a soup kettle; add the veal bones which have been cracked and 2 quarts of cold water. Cover and reduce until almost all the water has boiled away, leaving a sort of glaze. Add the calf's head, beef, onions, shallots, lemon rind and the seasoning and herbs, with water to cover generously and boil until the calf's head is done. Strain and let it cool; then remove all of the fat. Put back in the kettle, add the meat of the calf's head and the tongue cut in small cubes. Add the sherry and the lemon juice. Heat to the boiling point but do not boil.

Holy Saturday

In the early centuries of the Church, the lengthy office of Holy Saturday was recited at midnight on the eve of Easter. The ceremonies of the lighting of the new fire and illumination of the Paschal candle, the blessing of the baptismal font, and the prophecies and litanies ended, as was reasonable, at the first Mass of Easter morning itself. Today we have all this on the morning of Holy Saturday, but there are signs that we will return to the earlier way.

Lent is considered to end at noon on Holy Saturday. Not only is the fast ended, but there takes place the dropping of the veils from the statues, the swift replacing on the empty altar of candles and flowers in preparation for the glorious drama of the Resurrection.

The "anticipation" of Easter is observed in various countries on Holy Saturday by religious processions, the lighting of new fires and other local customs. Sometimes a large bonfire of burning logs is made before the cathedrals of Germany and Austria and used for the new fire of the liturgical ceremonies. From these the children take home pieces of burning wood, from which is lighted the fire for cooking the Easter food.

In Italian homes various customs are observed. The parish priest passes from house to house blessing each with holy water. At dinner the head of the family blesses the table with a palm branch kept from Palm Sunday, and special cakes and a *pizza* made with eggs are eaten.

Casatiella (Egg Pizza)

1 lb. flour
1 teaspoon salt
1 yeast cake
1 cup lukewarm water
2 tablespoons olive oil or lard
4 hard-boiled eggs

Sift flour and salt on a board and add the yeast which has been dissolved in the lukewarm water. Knead well and work in 2 tablespoons of olive oil or lard; knead again until smooth. Set aside in a warm place to rise for about three hours or until doubled in bulk. Then spread the dough about ¾ inch thick in your largest pie pan. Make eight holes at regular intervals, insert half a hard-boiled egg, and press surrounding dough over it to cover. Brush with a little oil or butter, sprinkle with salt, and bake for about twenty minutes in a 400° F. oven.

Most interesting customs are observed in Poland where the *Swiecone* or Easter repast is laid out in order on the table, sometimes enough food for the whole of Easter week, and blessed by the priest who makes the rounds to the homes of his flock on Holy Saturday. On this table one finds hams and legs of veal and lamb twined around with linked sausages. In the center is a mould of butter or a cake shaped like a lamb and circled with cakes and colored eggs. The moulded lamb is apt to carry a Polish flag—it is typical of Poland to bring the symbol of its beloved land to this great spiritual feast.

The Moravians brought early to this country from Bohemia by way of Germany their special observances of Holy Saturday. The Unitas Fratrum, or followers of Huss, settled in Pennsylvania in 1740, and at Bethlehem, Pennsylvania, among other places, their early customs are still faithfully observed.

In Bethlehem, in the late afternoon of Holy Saturday a band of trombone players mount to the steeple of the church, where traditional hymns are played. Afterward, following a "love feast," a choir, accompanied by the trombonists, goes from house to house singing, and this continues until early morning. After a breakfast of Moravian sugar cakes and coffee, the entire congregation returns to the church for a pre-sunrise meeting. Then in slow procession all go to the burial ground, where the graves of the departed have been decked with flowers; there, facing the east, the trombones greet the rising sun. There is a short service, and a very joyous one, for the Easter day has dawned.

Moravian Love Cakes

2 cups honey
2 tablespoons sugar
4 oz. chopped almonds
½ lb. chopped candied peel
½ teaspoon baking soda
½ teaspoon nutmeg
1 teaspoon cinnamon
pinch of cloves
rind of 1 lemon
2 tablespoons sherry or rum
flour

Boil the honey and sugar for five minutes. Add the chopped almonds and boil for another five minutes; then add the chopped candied peel, the soda, the nutmeg freshly

grated, cloves, cinnamon, lemon rind grated, and the sherry. Add enough sifted flour to make a dough that will roll out thinly, cut into oblongs, and bake in a 300° F. oven for about twenty minutes. Ice with sugar.

EASTER SUNDAY

Feast of the Resurrection

The greatest feast of the Christian Church takes its name, strangely enough, from that of Eastre, the Anglo-Saxon goddess of the dawn. For this statement we have the authority of the learned Venerable Bede.

The feast, however, has another name, the *Pasch,* the Greek word coming from the Hebrew *pesakh,* the Passover. This is the term for the feast which is used in nearly every language save English and German, and even these two use the words Paschal candle and Paschaltide. In the churches of the Eastern Orthodox the feast of Easter comes somewhat later than in the Western calendar, but the observance is as great, if not greater.

Among Orthodox Russians two people meeting on the street at Easter exchange greetings that give in two short phrases the essence of the day. "Christ is risen," says one, and the other responds, "He is risen indeed."

The Orthodox ceremony of Easter includes an early morning procession to a church which is in utter darkness; the Resurrection is announced to the congregation by the ceremony called "the Assault of Heaven," which takes place before its closed doors. Then the procession enters, but now into an edifice brilliantly lighted, for all know that Christ has, as the phrase has it, risen indeed.

In the older Russia Easter was a day of great feasting. On long tables were placed roasted pig and sausages and sweet tarts. And there was especially the *Paskha* of cheese and the *Koulich,* the latter a bread so delicate that pillows were put about the pan in which the dough was rising so that it would not fall; anxious housewives kept husbands with heavy boots and frolicking children out of the kitchen until the *Koulich* was safely out of the oven. Deep in the top of this cake were formed the letters "X V," the initials of the words meaning "Christ is risen."

Paskha

- ¾ lb. cream cheese
- ¼ lb. sweet butter
- ½ cup sour cream
- ¼ lb. sugar
- ¼ lb. chopped almonds
- ¼ lb. chopped candied peel
- ½ lb. seedless raisins

Take the cream cheese (or pot cheese) which should be quite dry and mix it well with the butter, sour cream, the sugar, the blanched, chopped almonds, the candied peel and the raisins. The mixing is essential and may best be done with an electric beater. Traditionally the *paskha* is pressed in a wooden mould. However, it can be placed in a strainer lined with a piece of moistened cheesecloth and left to drain for at least half a day or overnight. Turn out your *paskha* and decorate it with almonds and raisins in the form of a cross.

Koulich

- 1 cup white raisins
- 3 tablespoons rum
- 1½ yeast cakes
- ½ cup warm water
- 10 cups flour
- 1½ cups scalded milk
- 7 eggs
- 1 cup sugar
- ¾ lb. butter
- 1 teaspoon salt
- 1 teaspoon saffron

Soak the raisins in the rum. Soak the yeast in the lukewarm water. Mix 5 cups of the flour with the milk which has been cooled; combine with the yeast and beat well. Allow to rise for three hours in a warm place. Beat the yolks of 5 eggs with the sugar. Mix with the batter. Melt the butter, mix with the salt and the raisins, and add to the batter. Sift the rest of the flour with the saffron. Mix into the batter and knead well. Bake in a pan that should be about 12 inches high (a lard pail will do). Brush with butter and set to rise again till double in bulk. Brush top with egg yoke; bake in a 400° F. oven for fifteen minutes and then reduce heat to 350° F. for another forty-five minutes or until done.

The *Koulich* of Russia becomes the *Babka* of Poland; the name derives from the word meaning old woman, because the cake, tall and wide, looks like an old woman with wide skirts. For this feast the tables of Hungary were formerly as laden as those of Poland, and the various dishes served were very similar.

In Italy the Easter customs concerning food are many and varied. Even for breakfast are prepared special dishes of eggs with vegetables and herbs. There are many holiday breads, and on the dinner table appears inevitably *Agnellino* (roasted baby lamb) always accompanied by roasted artichokes.

Carciofi Arrostiti (Roasted Artichokes)

6 artichokes
2 tablespoons chopped parsley
2 cloves garlic, minced
salt and pepper
6 tablespoons olive oil
½ cup water

After removing the tough outer leaves of your artichokes, soak them for half an hour, heads down, in a bowl of well-salted cool water. Make a paste of your parsley, garlic, and salt and pepper and spread between the leaves of your artichokes. Place in a saucepan so that they will stand upright with half the oil at the bottom of the pan and the rest poured over the vegetables. "Roast" for five to six minutes over a high flame, taking care that they do not burn. Add a little water and cook until the water has evaporated. Then add the rest of the water and continue cooking, about half an hour in all, or until the outer leaves come off easily.

In Switzerland a plain coffee cake is made in the form of a small wreath in the center of which is imbedded a colored egg. When the baking is finished, the egg seems to be neatly resting in a brown nest. The custom also exists in Italy, but in bringing it to America the form of the cake has been changed. Often now we see it in the shape of a rabbit with colored eggs stuck in various places. This effect is ridiculous, but the little Swiss wreath is charming.

From Italy comes for this feast a wonderful soup called *Brodetto Pasquale.*

Brodetto Pasquale (Easter Broth)

1 lb. lean beef	3 leeks
1 lb. breast of lamb	herb bouquet
1 veal bone	spring marjoram
1 beef bone	peppercorns
3 qts. water	salt
3 carrots	egg yolks (1 per portion)
1 stalk celery	lemon juice

Parmesan cheese

Put the bones and the meat in the soup kettle with cold water. Bring to a boil and skim carefully. Add the vegetables, herbs and seasoning. Cover with a lid partially open (this helps to keep the broth clear) and simmer for about three hours. Break as many egg yolks in a dish as there are to be portions served and beat with a little lemon juice. Gradually add the soup, hot off the fire, stirring continuously. Place back on the fire and allow to thicken but *not* boil. Serve in a tureen, with narrow strips of toast dusted with grated Parmesan.

In Finland there is a very special Easter dish called *pääsiäsismämmi,* a porridge which from its name might well be called Proofreader's Despair, and from which even the trained and etymological eye can discern easily only the first part, evidently meaning Pasch. This porridge is as complicated as its name; it is made of rye flour, orange peel, and malt, and mixed with water, boiled very slowly, and eaten cold with cream. It is an indispensable Easter item on every Finnish table.

As in so many other lands, Greece prefers the lamb for Easter dinner to all other meats, though there is a very special bread called the Bread of Christ, marked with a cross and decorated with red Easter eggs, which is also a required item. But the important thing is lamb. In fact, there comes from Macedonia this proverb, "Easter without lamb is a thing that cannot be."

Greek Easter Lamb

Prepare your leg of lamb as usual. When it is ready for the oven, make three or four incisions and insert in each a clove of garlic. Rub with salt and pepper, lemon juice, and a generous portion of marjoram. Wild marjoram is used in Greece and is called *rigano*. If you can get dried *orégano,* use this instead of the marjoram. In Greek *origanon* means "the joy of the mountains." Since leg of lamb is inclined to be dry, most cooks advise leaving the skin, or fell, around it. However, then the seasoning does not penetrate as well as it should. Should your lamb be dry, rub it well with 2 tablespoons of butter before applying the seasoning. Lamb should be well done, in a moderate oven, and basted from time to time with the pan juices. It may be served with rice or potatoes or eggplant. If using potatoes, slice them thin and add them to the roast, with a cup of tomatoes, half an hour before the roast is done. If using rice, this may also be added to the roasting pan but see that it has been cooked for about ten minutes previously; instead of tomatoes, use 2 cups of tomato juice which will be absorbed by the rice. Small eggplants, cut in half lengthwise (do not peel), can be added with the potatoes and tomatoes. The roasting time depends upon the size of your leg of lamb, but thirty to thirty-five minutes to the pound will suffice.

To the lamb Greece adds jellied fish in a cross-shaped mould, *Dolmas* and *Callalou* and a delicious rose leaf jam.

Rose Leaf Jam

Take the petals only of dark red roses, taking care not to include any of the pollen, and an equal amount of sugar. To a pound of each allow the juice of 2 lemons and a little water. Set in the sun until the sugar is completely melted. Then boil for twenty minutes and put in jars.

Not in any one country but in nearly every land we find another specific article of food for this day, and that is the Easter egg. The coloring of eggs for spring festivals is a very ancient custom and long pre-dates Christianity. The Egyptians and the Persians, the Greeks and the Romans, all colored eggs. In every land the egg is the symbol of fertility; the coloring on them is sometimes merely adornment but sometimes it has a deeper meaning, as in countries where they are colored red as a symbol of the blood of Christ.

In Poland colored eggs are called *pisanki*, from the word to write, because the Easter egg is one on which are written symbols. Perhaps the most beautiful of all are the diagramed eggs of the Russians, works of true art and almost too beautiful to be broken and eaten in plebeian fashion.

The Easter eggs one sees today in many homes in the United States are not the colored eggs of an earlier day. The little pellets pasted on a card and dissolved in old cups are too pastel for some of us oldsters. We remember eggs that were far from pallid as these are, and that were, in fact, exactly like the vivid foreign eggs.

One of us remembers how her mother made her own dyes. She boiled the skins of yellow onions for hours and produced with the liquid glorious orange eggs. She made the red ones by boiling red yarn in water. The green came from little bottles of color bought at the drug store, but occasionally she made this too from young spinach, washed, squeezed, and boiled. Often these colors were dappled on the hot egg with a new lampwick. And then, while they were still hot, all the eggs were rubbed with a cloth dipped in butter. These bright shells were, as Browning says somewhere, "reds and greens indeed." The pastel product of today is too pale and insipid for those who remember the vivid bowls of eggs in the center of the dining room table.

These early American eggs and the fine ones in Slavic countries are the only Easter eggs worthy of consideration —the marvelously designed and intricately drawn Russian one and the old-fashioned and deeply colored American egg. But never the heresy of one with a bunny stamped on it; never the pallid copy made with pellet dyes; and never the ones whose insides have been blown out through a pin hole with the shell only surviving as a symbol. Symbol indeed! The symbol is a bright egg which is to be eaten and enjoyed, a well-cooked egg which is also a delight to the palate.

APRIL 23

Feast of Saint George

Among saints honored in the month of April there is Saint George, of whom little is known, for all his popularity, except that he was born in Cappadocia, that he was a soldier and suffered martyrdom. The crusaders brought his fame to the West, where he is the patron of England, Aragon, Portugal, and certain sections of Germany. Before the Conquest many English churches had been named for him and the story of his brave deeds was sung everywhere.

His best-known deed is legendary, but it was of course his slaying of the dragon, a feat he carried out in order to save a maiden who had been vowed to a monster. Saint George transfixed the dragon with a spear and then told the maiden to lead the monster about the city, after which he put an end to him. He was well known by that time as a man of God and a confessor of His works, and on that day, after witnessing the miraculous slaying of the dragon, twenty thousand people were converted to Christ.

The king begged this wonderful dragon slayer to stay, "If you will remain with us you shall have the half of my kingdom." But Saint George refused the fine offer. "I must ride on," he said, "to take care of God's churches and honor the clergy and have pity on the poor."

Saint George is especially honored in England as its great patron, and flags are still floated there on his feast; in other times the celebration was more elaborate and processions, jousts and races were held. The dishes served on this day should be without doubt favorites of that country such as roast beef and its famous accompaniment, Yorkshire pudding.

Roast Beef

Have the roast at room temperature about an hour before cooking. Season with salt and pepper and dredge with flour. Preheat the oven to 300° F. and place the roast, fat side up, in a roasting pan. Should the roast be very lean, cover with a thin strip of suet or salt pork. Roast at this temperature allowing about eighteen minutes to the pound for rare, twenty-two minutes for medium, and thirty minutes for a well-done roast. If the roast has been boned and rolled, allow an additional five minutes per pound in the cooking time. Formerly the Yorkshire pudding was cooked in the same pan with the roast. But it is best to cook it in a separate pan since we now roast beef at a much slower temperature than formerly.

Yorkshire Pudding

1 cup flour	1 cup milk
2 eggs	½ teaspoon salt

Make a smooth batter of the flour, eggs, milk, and salt. Twenty minutes before the roast is done, remove from the pan and pour off half the grease for gravy. Pour the batter into the pan, place a wire rack over it, set the roast on the rack, and return it to the oven until the Yorkshire Pudding

is well crisped around the edges. Cut into squares. Arrange the roast on a platter. Serve with gravy. There is an old rule that Worcestershire sauce should be added, 1 drop for chicken and veal, 3 for beef and lamb, 5 for pork.

In Allier, a winegrowing *département* of France, where the vineyards are objects of great solicitude, a curious custom is observed on Saint George's Day. If frost has not touched before that date the precious vines, a clean, soft little towel is offered to the statue of the saint and his feet are washed in wine amid cries of "*Vive Monsieur Saint Georges.*" If harm has befallen the vineyards, however, Saint George is not so popular, and though his feet are still washed, a rough, coarse cloth is used.

APRIL 25

Feast of Saint Mark

One other well-known saint of this month is Mark, a favorite disciple and companion of Saint Paul. He founded the first church in Alexandria and was slain by pagans of that city. For years his tomb was a shrine for the faithful but, according to tradition, in 815 a Venetian trader buying wares in Alexandria obtained the body of Saint Mark and brought it to Venice. And there it is today in the great cathedral in the city of which he is patron.

On this day in Hungary people go in procession to have the fields of wheat blessed. And on the return home each carries a sprout of wheat, which has been blessed so that "fog shall not strangle, hail shall not destroy, storm shall not trample, fire shall not consume the only hope of the people."

Since Saint Mark is so particularly honored in Venice, where the specialities are such seafood as sea trout, eels, sole, shrimp and sturgeon, we suggest an excellent Venetian fish sauce for this day.

Venetian Sauce

1 tablespoon flour
½ cup butter
½ cup meat stock
½ cup fish stock
1 tablespoon chopped parsley
pinch of white pepper

Blend the flour in half the melted butter in a saucepan; add the meat and fish stocks, mixing well and cooking for about five minutes. Add pepper and the rest of the butter, beating constantly. When all is well mingled, add the parsley and serve with boiled fish.

APRIL 30

Saint Walburga's Eve

The last day of April was first celebrated as a druidic feast of some importance in honor of spring's return, and bonfires were lighted to frighten away the spirits of darkness which might prevent the arrival of the joyous goddess of the springtide. For Christians it became the feast of Saint Walburga, the daughter of a Saxon king of the eighth century, who went to Germany at the call of her uncle, Saint Boniface, to aid in the work of evangelizing the Germanic tribes and remained to found and rule monasteries and convents. The Abbess of Heidenheim was given great veneration in the Low Countries and Germany during her lifetime and was honored after her death for her learning and the many miracles she wrought. But the observance of her feast, or rather its eve, *Walpurgisnacht*, came to be held with many of the pagan traditions peculiar to the day, so that it grew to resemble the celebration of Halloween. At its best, it is the night when protection is invoked against murrains of fields and crops and the spirits of evil; at its worst, it is a night when witches ride and dark deeds are done.

The original pagan feast, celebrated as the Eve of

Beltane in the British Isles, was accompanied by lighting of new fires and feasting on certain foods retained by later customs in Scotland, Wales, and Ireland. We are told that Beltane Cakes, large and scalloped, were set against hot stones to bake while a caudle (custard) was eaten, and beer and whiskey consumed. Many customs were connected with these cakes, among them that the person drawing a piece blackened by the fire became the "carline" who must be sacrificed to the fire. Later in Wales when cakes were cooked on ordinary stoves, light and dark oatmeal cakes were made, and the one who drew the dark cake was required to jump three times through the flames of the lighted bonfire.

We have been unable to trace any authentic recipes for Beltane Cakes, and everyone knows how to make a custard or caudle. However, on this eve one might well anticipate the day to come by brewing the first *Maibowle*.

Maibowle

Take 1 quart of strawberries, washed and hulled, sprinkle them with several tablespoons of powdered sugar, and steep them in 1 quart of good white wine. After three or four hours, place the berries and their liquor in a large punch bowl, place a large piece of ice in the center, and pour in 3 more bottles of white wine and 1 bottle of champagne. (The champagne can be replaced by soda water.) There are many classic and traditional *bowlen* in Germany, and peaches, pineapple, or *waldmeister* (woodruff) may be used instead of strawberries. Serve with a bit of the fruit in each punch glass.

MAY 1

May Day

The first day of May has been for centuries a beloved holiday in England where "bringing in the May" has been sung by poets great and small. In France May is called *le mois de Marie,* in honor of Our Lady; it is the month of First Communions, of solemn little boys in Sunday suits and little girls in white dresses and veils, all walking in procession to the churches. Yet, for all the devotions to Mary with which this month is filled not only in France but in many other countries, it remains for many the first day of the month when spring has come to stay.

Originally May 1st was a Roman festival dedicated to Flora, the spring goddess who in Greece was known as Maia. Ever since the Romans brought their *Floralia* to the isles of Britain, England's celebrations of May Day have been the most elaborate. After Britain became a Christian land and Whitsuntide had replaced the celebration to Flora, it was easy to continue the pleasant old customs of Maypoles and May dances on the green, of May Queens and processions, all so joyous that it made Spenser sing:

To see these folks mak such a joyissance
Made my heart after the pipes to dance.

Despite the fact that much feasting and many joyful customs were exiled from Merrie England by the followers of Calvin and Cromwell, they could not take away this celebration from the British, nor could the solemn men who came to America to found New England. Right before the eyes of Governor Bradford who called it "an idoll Maypole," one such pole was set up in 1628 in Plymouth Colony, and the young people celebrated in a way described by a chronicler as the dancing of "good May songs, dancing hand in hand around the Maypole and performing exercises in a solemn manner, with revels and merriment after the old English custom." The proceedings were altered a bit to fit Puritan decorum, but the important thing was that May Day was being celebrated still, and in the New World. Those who have been born in Arcady must return there for at least one day of the year to keep the spirit and the heart alive.

And ever since the *Floralia* when Romans gathered spring blossoms to offer to their goddess, flowers have figured preponderantly in the May Day celebration. In France *muguets*, lilies of the valley, are worn and sent to friends to wish them luck—the saying goes that a wish made while wearing these fragrant blossoms will come true. And these flowers, carefully pressed and dried, are sent to make known good wishes to faraway friends and loved ones.

In the America of some forty years ago we remember that on May Day children made little baskets, often woven with strips of paper or raffia, filled them with flowers from the woods—trillium and bloodroot, violets purple and white, adder's-tongues, anemones. Only to repeat the names of these blossoms brings back the memory of days when we filled May baskets, hung them on the doorknobs at the homes of our friends, and then ran home to find others on our own door.

Round about Paris on May Day morning one still drinks May milk, which is thought to be better than in other months. Russians decorate birch trees with streamers and flowers, and sometimes eggs and meat pies are set beneath the trees. In the celebrations of the South Germans there are customs involving the planting of trees and Maypoles, and in some sections eggs, sausages, and cakes are hidden in the branches. A traditional luncheon or breakfast dish is *Bauernfrühstück.*

Bauernfrühstück (Peasant Breakfast)

3 strips bacon
1 boiled potato
1 egg
salt and pepper
chives

Cut the bacon in small pieces and fry over a low flame until completely done. Cube the potato and brown with the bacon. Finally, break an egg over the whole (do not beat previously) and stir it slowly into the bacon and potato until set. Season and sprinkle with finely cut chives. This is for one portion and can be multiplied at will.

We find certain traditional May dishes in our own United States. In Maryland it is customary to serve hot rolls for breakfast on May 1st. In New England "Baptist Cakes" are eaten. These are made of bread pulled from the loaf dough and patted into balls, fried in a pan, and served with maple syrup.

Ascension Thursday

This day falls on the fortieth day after Easter when Christ disappeared from view of His followers—"and a cloud received Him out of their sight." In addition to its religious observance there are many customs and even superstitions connected with this feast, to insure good crops and good luck.

In Rome a fine custom was observed not so long ago on the feast of the Ascension: the milkman brought a gift of milk and rennet to his customers, and from this was made *Giuncata.* The recipe sounds exactly like the junket we make from little tablets and which, when properly cooled, is a favorite dessert for children. The Roman recipe however contains an addition that takes this out of the children's class and makes it more interesting for grown-ups. The Romans add to it sugar and rum or brandy. Whether anyone on this side of the Atlantic has thought of doing this or dismissed junket as an insipid dish we do not know.

In parts of France on Ascension Day, children go around begging for flour to make *Beignets.*

Beignets de Pommes (Apple Fritters)

2 eggs	2 cups flour
½ teaspoon salt	1 cup milk
1 tablespoon brandy	4 apples

Work the egg yolks together with the salt and brandy into your flour until all is thoroughly mixed. Add the milk and stir until smooth. Beat the egg whites until stiff and fold into the batter. Peel and core the apples and cut into thin rounds. Dip apple in batter and fry from four to five minutes in deep fat at 375° F. Dust with sugar or serve with a soft custard, or vanilla sauce. Apricots, bananas, peaches, pineapples, or plums may be substituted for the apples.

MAY 19

Feast of Saint Ives

Sancto Yvo erat Brito,
Advocatus et non latro
Res miranda populo.

So runs the popular verse in Brittany, where in the thirteenth century Saint Ives followed the profession of lawyer and judge with distinction, as the verse says of him:

Lo! a marvel past belief,
A barrister who's not a thief!

Although possessed of wealth, he lived as a Franciscan tertiary, dressed in coarse clothing, and cared for the poor and unfortunate, keeping, it is said, up to seven orphans in his family manor of Kermartin. His benefactions to the poor continued after his death, and it is not surprising that his feast is observed in Brittany by one of the many Pardons or local religious pilgrimages of this Celtic part of France called the Pardon of the Poor at Minihy.

After his death, Saint Ives' manor was left to the poor, and here they continued to come especially on the eve and day of his feast. We read that on one occasion in the nineteenth century so many beggars presented themselves that no one knew how they would be fed. But no matter how much was dipped out of the kettles on the hearth, they were always found filled to the brim with good, nourishing soup.

No record is made of just what went into these kettles, but in honor of Saint Ives, the saint of the poor and the patron of (reformed?) lawyers, we suggest *Potage Paysanne.*

Potage Paysanne (Peasant Soup)

2 carrots
2 potatoes
2 leeks
1 turnip
¼ head cabbage
6 cups stock
stale bread
salt and pepper

Dice the carrots, potatoes, leeks, and turnip and cut the cabbage into slivers; cook in 2 cups of the stock until the vegetables are done. Add the remaining stock and boil for ten minutes. Take rounds of stale French bread and brown them a bit in the oven, place in a tureen and pour the soup over them.

Pentecost or Whitsunday

In the Jewish calendar Pentecost, meaning "fiftieth day," marks the Feast of Weeks or "the fiftieth day from the next day after the Passover." In the same way the Christian festival celebrates the fiftieth day after Easter, for we remember that the Resurrection was closely connected with the feast of the Passover.

For the Christian world this is a major feast and one of rejoicing, for the descent of the Paraclete in tongues of fire strengthened the faith and courage of the Apostles and insured the future of Christianity. As a Christian feast it dates back to the first century, and in early times catechumens in their white robes were baptized on this day; hence our English name of Whitsunday. In Italy, however, it is also known as *Pascha rossa* because the vestments worn at Mass on this Sunday are red. In other parts of the same country, especially Sicily, Pentecost has still another name, *Pascha rosarum,* because rose leaves are scattered from the ceilings of the churches to commemorate the miracle of the tongues.

All through Western Europe this feast was greatly celebrated in medieval times. In France a sequence to the Mass of the day was written by King Robert. Trumpets were blown during the religious ceremonies to symbolize the roaring of the winds as the Holy Spirit descended upon the Apostles. Law courts were forbidden to sit for an entire week and little servile work was done.

In England during the reign of King Arthur there were magnificent tournaments at Whitsuntide. Miracle or mystery plays were given, and we learn that Roswitha, the celebrated nun-poetess of the tenth century, wrote one of these, performed at Chester.

Many other customs grew up in England around this feast. English farmers gave milk on this day to all who asked for it. "Smoke money" was paid to the church, based on the number of chimneys on the house owned. There were morris dances in every parish, and the old looked on while the young danced; everyone ate the food he had brought and purchased "Whitsun ale." Shakespeare had doubtless this in mind when he wrote:

It hath been sung at festivals,
On ember eves and holy ales.

The Whitsun Ales, so called by the people, had their origin in the agapae or love feasts of the early Christians, and the drink was made by the churchwardens who bought the malt and brewed it in advance. The profits of these Ales were given to the poor, according to a Christian rule that all profits would be spent in alms.

In addition to ale, custards, cheese cakes, and huge roasts were typical of this feast in England, and another favored dish was Gooseberry Pudding.

Gooseberry Pudding

3 cups gooseberries
1 cup bread crumbs
3 tablespoons butter
4 tablespoons sugar
3 eggs
short pastry

Top, tail, and wash the gooseberries. Cook them in a light sugar syrup until done and then press them through a sieve. Add the bread crumbs, butter, sugar and beaten eggs. Line the edges of a dish with a good short pastry, pour in the mixture, and bake at 375° F. for about forty minutes.

Whitsuntide is also observed in various sections of the United States, and in New York St. George's Church holds a fair annually on this day.

JUNE 8

Feast of Saint Medard

Should Saint Medard's day be wet
It will rain for forty yet;
At least until Saint Barnabas
The summer sun won't favor us,

is a saying in France, and particularly in Picardy where Saint Medard was born in Merovingian times. He was bishop of Noyon and a great missionary who worked for the conversion of the Franks. When Queen Radegunde left her murderer-husband, King Clotaire, she fled to Medard for refuge and was clothed by him in the religious habit.

The stories of how he became a "weather saint" are many and varied. One day, says the legend, Saint Medard gave away one of his father's finest colts to a poor peasant who had lost his horse. Immediately after this took place there was a torrential rain, and everyone was soaked to the skin except the generous youth. "It is Saint Medard watering his colts," say the French farmers when the June rains come and help up their work. Later, when he was a bishop, Saint Medard was known for his kindness to the farming people and especially to the poor among them.

He set aside the income from twelve acres of his own land to be given to the most virtuous girl of his diocese, and it was he who started the "feast of the rose queen." For many centuries in French churches a crown of roses was placed upon the head of the girl who had most edified the parish. The custom of crowning the rose queen still exists in some of the working districts in the suburbs of Paris, but the feast has become a secular one and takes place in the local *salle des fêtes* with the mayor and civil officials in attendance.

Rose Potpourri

½ oz. violet powder	½ teaspoon cloves
1 oz. orrisroot	4 drops oil of roses
½ oz. rose powder	10 drops chiris
½ oz. heliotrope powder	20 drops oil melisane
½ teaspoon mace	20 drops oil eucalyptus
¼ teaspoon cinnamon	10 drops bergamot

2 drams alcohol

Gather rose petals when the roses are in their richest bloom, but not when the dew is on them, and pack in a jar in layers two inches deep, sprinkling about two tablespoons of fine, dry salt upon each layer. Continue this until the jar is full, adding fresh petals and salt daily. Keep in a dark, dry, cool place. A week after the last relay is gathered turn out the salted petals upon a broad platter, mix and toss together until the mass is loosened. Then incorporate thoroughly with the ingredients given above; pack in a clean jar, cover lightly, and set away to "ripen." It will be ready for rose jars, etc., in a fortnight, and, if kept covered, will be good and fragrant for twenty years.

JUNE 9

Feast of Saint Columba

A long-ago saint whose feast comes in June is Saint Columba, a missionary from Ireland to the Picts, a name given to the Scots in the sixth century. He was in his forty-fourth year when with twelve companians he crossed the sea in a *curragh*, a boat of wickerwork covered with hides, and landed at Iona on the eve of Pentecost in the year 563.

He spent most of the remaining years of his life among the inhabitants of the glens and straths of northern Scotland. The stories of him that have come down to us show him a kind and gentle man who founded many monasteries and churches and got along well with the Scottish shepherds and sheep raisers. When he died it was at the foot of the altar before which he had spent much of his life.

On his day, even at the present time in various parts of Scotland, an oaten cake is baked in his honor, and in the dough is placed a silver coin. To the child who receives the coin in his share of the cake goes the honor of being put in charge of the new lambs for the next twelve months, an office very popular with small shepherds.

The cake to which we refer is known as a Bannock from the Gaelic *bannach*, meaning a cake; that is, a large round scone or oatcake. It is a thing of substance and may be made of oatmeal, wheat, or barley flour. We give here a popular variety.

Bannock

- 2 oz. almonds
- 1 lb. flour
- 4 tablespoons sugar
- 2 oz. candied orange peel
- ½ lb. butter

Blanch and shred the almonds and mix them with the flour, sugar, and orange peel on a pastry board. Make a well in the center into which put the butter and knead until it is well blended. Roll out and form into round cakes, pinching the edges, and prick the centers with a fork. Bake on a greased baking sheet in a 375° F. oven for one hour.

JUNE 13

Feast of Saint Anthony

Few are the saints more beloved and invoked than Saint Anthony of Padua. A Franciscan of the twelfth century, many of his achievements have been forgotten because of his reputation as a saint who has the special ability to help find things which have been lost. Despite the humility that made him sweep each day the floor of the monastery and slow to speak for himself, he was an eloquent and stern preacher against error, so much so that he was known as the "hammer of heretics." He could speak many languages, and evidently all his sermons were not of the fiery kind, for we are told that even the fishes listened to him with delight.

In statues we see him holding the Infant Jesus, because of a vision he had of the Child, his devotion to whom no doubt had much to do with making him the helpful, kindly saint he is to the world today. Lighted tapers are always to be found burning before his statue and altar in churches. In fact, so much is he appealed to, that it is sometimes hard to find a candle unlighted—so many, many things go astray in this world.

Saint of the lost, who may not stay nor stand
While one child wanders from his mother's hand,

wrote one modern poet of him. He is reputed able to find anything, from money and papers and jewelry to lost children, from lost gloves to lost love.

There are some who feel that he does too much, especially when he retrieves the belongings of careless people whose possessions should perhaps justly stay lost because they take no care of them, but evidently this is not Saint Anthony's code.

Dear Saint Anthony, please come round —
Something is lost and must be found,

runs another rhyme.

For his feast day we suggest a dish with a name we are sure would delight his heart, for no doubt a saint who finds lost things for people must be one saint who hates waste of any kind. We refer to *Pain Perdu,* which is made of stale rolls.

Pain Perdu (Lost Bread)

6 rolls
2 cups milk
2 tablespoons sugar
2 egg yolks
butter

Take rolls that are stale and grate off all of the crust, setting aside the crumbs. Divide the rolls in two and soak them in the milk which has been mixed with the sugar. After about fifteen minutes, take them out and squeeze them gently. Dip them in the beaten egg yolks and then in the crumbs grated from the crusts. Fry them a light brown in butter and serve with sugar and cinnamon, currant jelly, or a vanilla sauce.

JUNE 24

Feast of Saint John the Baptist

The great feast of this month, one common to many lands and celebrated since very early times, is the Nativity of Saint John the Baptist, also known as Midsummer. In many places bonfires are lighted in Saint John's honor, just as long before the Christian era fires were lighted on this day to celebrate the summer solstice. Especially in Ireland and in England these bonfires had their origin in the Druidic fires lighted in honor of the god of the sacred wood. But today they are everywhere known as the Fires of Saint John, although a few pagan customs remain in connection with the celebration. When the lassies of Ireland and Poland drop melted lead into cold water to foretell their future, they are following a custom that stems from the Druidic methods of soothsaying.

In Finland the cities are all but empty on Saint John's Eve for everyone is out in the country celebrating the Midsummer or Saint John's festival. Of course in many places no pagan or even secular meaning is attached to the feast. In France the bonfires are built as close as possible to one of Saint John's own chapels. It is considered important that a lad named Jean or a girl named Jeanne provide a wreath to throw onto the fire. When vesper services are over, the priest kindles the blaze, and the evening is given over to dancing and singing which last till far into the night.

In Germany the more daring of the young men leap through the *Johannesfeuer*, and sometimes in Hungary betrothed couples leap through the flames together; if they succeed without being parted they know they will always remain together, and to make their success sure, the rest of the company dances about the two and sings:

May God send a slow shower
To wash these two together
Like two golden twigs.

In Mexico Saint John's feast is his and his alone, and the summer solstice has no slightest share in it. He is the Mexicans' dearly beloved saint, especially the saint of waters; and on his day wells and fountains are bright with ribbons and flowers. At midnight on the eve, everyone bathes: in the country in lake or pool or river; in large cities the festivities center around the fashionable bathhouses where swimming contests and exhibitions of diving skill take place.

Saint John's Day in Mexico is definitely also a day of feasting. Everyone brings food to the bathing places—cakes and sweets, but also chicken tamales and stuffed peppers, pork *tacos* and *empanadas*.

Tortillas de Harina (Flour Tortillas)

2 cups flour	1 tablespoon lard
1 teaspoon salt	cold water

Sift flour and salt together and cut in the lard and sufficient cold water to make a stiff dough. Knead on a floured board, divide into small balls and roll out to ⅛-inch thickness. Cook on a lightly greased griddle.

Tacos

½ lb. lean pork
4 tablespoons lard
2 onions
1 green pepper
6 tomatoes
1 tablespoon raisins
3 tablespoons sherry
1 hard-boiled egg
tortillas
grated cheese

Grind the pork and fry it in 2 tablespoons of the lard. Grind 1 onion, the pepper, and 1 tomato and add to the meat. Simmer for a few minutes and then add the raisins, the sherry, and the mashed boiled egg. Cook the second onion with the remaining tomatoes in 2 tablespoons of lard and add enough water to make a good sauce. Simmer for about ten minutes. Moisten each tortilla in the sauce, place a tablespoon of the meat mixture on each, and roll it up. Place tortillas in a greased baking dish, cover with the sauce, sprinkle with grated cheese, and bake in a 375° F. oven until the cheese is melted.

Empanadas de Orno (Meat Pies)

3 onions
1 green pepper
butter
1 lb. ground beef
½ can niblet corn
½ can cream corn
½ cup ripe olives
½ cup raisins
salt and pepper
pie dough
2 hard-boiled eggs

Chop onions and pepper and fry in a little butter until they begin to brown. Then add the meat and fry for about ten minutes. Add the corn, the pitted ripe olives, and raisins, with salt and pepper to taste. Roll out your favorite pie dough and cut into rounds. Place a tablespoon of the mixture on each, lay a slice of hard-boiled egg on top; fold pastry over and pinch the edges. Sprinkle brown sugar on top and bake in a 400° F. oven until done.

In Spain many are content to walk through the dew on Saint John's Eve, but others bathe in the sea; there are the usual bonfires and fortunetelling, and heart-shaped cakes are purchased by every swain for his señorita.

In Latvia carolers, singing the praises of the saint, go from door to door on Saint John's Eve, quite as they do on Christmas Eve. To have the singers come in and give the household a special concert is considered a high honor, and the singers are openly lured to enter. As the group approaches a house, the enterprising housewife stands holding out to them bread and cheese, and behind her, her husband offers mugs full of a sweet light beer, made especially for the occasion.

In England a similar custom prevailed for many years: on Saint John's Eve householders in towns and villages called to passers-by to stop for a bite and a sip. In some places the bread and cheese and beer were placed on little tables outside the front door. We highly approve this idea of having people stop for a little hospitality, whether they are strangers in town or old friends, and we think the old English custom sounds wonderfully inviting in lieu of cocktail parties in tight airless rooms.

Some food connected with Saint John has always had a doubtful sound to many of us. We read that John himself when in the desert fed on locusts and wild honey. The latter seems fine, the other not so good. But etymologists tell us these locusts were not bugs but beans; in fact in the Southwest of the United States there is a bean called *algarroba*, in common parlance locust beans. With much relief, remembering an early Sunday school vision of Saint John crunching grasshoppers which even wild honey could not have rendered palatable, we accept this pleasanter version.

JUNE 29

Feast of Saint Peter

The last day but one of this month celebrates the feast of Saint Peter. Mrs. Jameson in her monumental work,

Sacred and Legendary Art, says that "all saints are, in one sense, patron saints; either as protectors of some particular nation, province or city, or of some particular avocation, trade, or condition of life; but there is a wide distinction to be drawn between the merely national and local saints, and those universally accepted and revered." Surely Saint Peter belongs in the latter category.

Peter is usually depicted as a robust man, of undaunted countenance: he is given the broad rustic features befitting a pilot of the Galilean Sea and is shown with a short, curled beard and a bald head.

One of the badges of Saint Peter is the cock, an allusion to the crowing of that bird which caused the saint to go out and weep bitterly for his denial of Christ; but when he is distinguished by a fish, the symbol is of double significance—Peter's avocation as a fisherman and his mission as a fisher of men.

In many sea-coast towns of England he is regarded as chief protector and his day made one of high festival. Boats are decked in ribbons and flowers and often repainted in honor of the occasion. Races and feats of seamanship take place before an admiring crowd on shore, and everyone gathers together for a feast of which the chief dish is always fish.

Fillet of Flounder in Tomato Sauce

- 4 flounder fillets
- 1 onion
- 1 green pepper
- butter
- 6 tomatoes
- 2 tablespoons flour
- 3 tablespoons cream

Mince the onion and green pepper and cook in a little butter till soft. Cut up the tomatoes and add to the onion and pepper. Simmer for about ten minutes. Stir the flour to a paste with the cream, add to the sauce, and cook a bit longer. If too dry, a little more tomato juice may be added. Bring to a boil, put in your fillets and cook for about ten minutes.

JULY 4

Independence Day

THIS MONTH holds for Americans the celebration of our glorious Fourth, Independence Day, a great national holiday not connected with the feast of a saint (as is Saint Andrew's Day in Scotland and Saint George's in England), or with a festival of the Church. And yet can it be said that the anniversary of the birth of a nation is ever an entirely secular affair? In this case we do not believe it is so. In man's aspirations for freedom, there is always a spiritual element, and this was especially true in the thinking of the American signers of the Declaration of Independence at Philadelphia on July 4, 1776. On Thanksgiving Day we give thanks to God that He has provided our citizens with food for the body; at this other particularly American celebration we give thanks that He has allowed our spirit to live.

For years the Fourth of July has been marked in every city and town of the United States by patriotic gatherings, parades, and speechmaking in the principal square; the national anthem and other songs are sung (which sound especially well when shrilled by young and untrained voices); and martial airs are played by the local band. But the firecrackers of our childhood are no more, a pity and a blessing too. The slogan of a safe and sane Fourth is now becoming a fixed rule everywhere, and in these days the fireworks are set off at night by competent and careful manipulators.

Last Independence Day we attended such a display—one of many thousands throughout the country—and sat on a hilltop watching the fireworks. Around us children chattered and lighted sparklers; when some particularly dazzling skyrocket burst red and blue and white against the night sky, there was clapping from the crowd. Last of all appeared the usual "set piece"—the American flag with Roman candles clustered about it.

All stood up as a voice in the crowd began "The Star Spangled Banner"; the singing grew louder and louder as more people joined in. The peaceful evening and the rockets' harmless glare, the voices of free people singing a free song, the knowledge that that freedom had been defended in the past and might have to be defended again on nights far from peaceful and with weapons far from harmless—all produced an emotion that could perhaps be called sentimental. But devotion to the truth that made us free, and alone will keep us free, was still there, right in the midst of the sentiment.

Independence Day food is often of the picnic variety, as is right for a holiday usually spent in the open. But there are traditional dishes originating in George Washington's Virginia. One such is a breakfast specialty, Rice Waffles.

Rice Waffles

2 egg yolks
1 cup milk
1 cup flour
1 cup hot boiled rice
4 tablespoons melted butter
2 egg whites

Mix the egg yolks with the milk; add the flour, rice, and melted butter. Finally fold in the stiffly beaten egg whites. Bake as usual and serve with the following sauce:

Sauce for Rice Waffles

½ lb. strained honey	2 teaspoons cinnamon
½ cup maple syrup	caraway seeds

Beat together thoroughly ½ pound of strained honey and ½ cup of maple syrup and heat slowly in a double boiler. Add 2 teaspoons of cinnamon and a few grains of caraway seeds. Serve hot.

Another dish of the day is poached salmon with egg and caper sauce, served with green peas and mashed potatoes. Not only is this the traditional time for serving the first salmon of the season, but we learn that this menu of soft foods was prepared for the Father of our country because of the discomfort caused him by his ill-fitting set of false teeth!

Poached Salmon

1 cup white wine	4 sprigs parsley
2 qts. water	2 shallots
2 tablespoons vinegar	6 peppercorns
2 chopped onions	1 clove garlic
2 carrots	2 whole cloves
1 stalk celery	salt

salmon

Bring the wine and water to a boil. (It is classic to use half wine and half water but this may prove too expensive for most pockets.) Add the vinegar, the vegetables, and spices and simmer gently for about half an hour before adding the fish. Unless you have a fish boiler it is advisable to wrap your salmon in a piece of cheesecloth to facilitate handling. Simmer, never boil, the fish, allowing twelve minutes to the pound. Remove skin and serve on a warm platter.

Egg and Caper Sauce

4 tablespoons butter
4 tablespoons flour
2 cups hot milk
½ cup heavy cream
2 hard-boiled eggs
2 tablespoons capers
2 tablespoons chopped parsley
few drops lemon juice
pinch of salt
pinch of paprika

Melt the butter and gradually stir in the flour and cook for several minutes. Then add the hot milk and stir constantly until the sauce is thick. Add the cream, the chopped hard boiled eggs, capers (carefully drained), parsley, lemon juice and finally the salt and paprika. Stir until smooth and serve hot.

And of course the day's dessert everywhere has long been a triangle or a circle of watermelon. Never, never, we hope, will it become the small new variety just developed, we hear with a sense of shock, with no seeds at all. The color combination surely should all be kept in the true watermelon—the black seeds, with the red, the white, and the green.

Further, we hear, the experts are working not only to produce a seedless watermelon, but one with a very thin green rind. When that happens, what will happen to one of the nation's delicacies, the watermelon pickle? Before that dread day, we hasten to offer here a recipe for this truly American relish:

Watermelon Pickle

rind of 1 large watermelon
salted water
4 cups water
8 cups sugar
4 cups cider vinegar
4 teaspoons whole cloves
4 teaspoons whole allspice
8 sticks cinnamon

Peel and remove all the green and pink portions from the rind of 1 large watermelon. Cut into squares, oblongs, or any desired shape and soak in salt water to cover, allowing 1 tablespoon of salt to 1 cup of water. Soak for about twelve hours or overnight. Drain, cover with fresh water, and cook gently until almost tender. Make a syrup of the water, sugar, vinegar, and spices (tied in a cheesecloth bag) and boil for about twenty minutes. Remove the spice bag, add the drained watermelon, and cook until clear and transparent. Pack at once in sterilized jars and seal.

Another dessert in favor on the Fourth of July from the very beginning of these United States is the Independence Day Cake. This very properly had its origin in Philadelphia, and every heirloom cookery book has its recipe. Tall and frosted in white, it is surrounded with a wreath of gilded leaves, made in early days of the boxwood so popular in colonial hedges. It is a cake of victory, of snowy purity, its wreath reflecting the gold of the seal of the Declaration, well suited to a day which made this a free land for free men.

Independence Day Cake

1 yeast cake	1½ cups sugar
¼ cup lukewarm water	3 eggs
4½ cups sifted flour	1 jigger sherry
1½ teaspoons cinnamon	1 jigger brandy
1½ teaspoons cloves	3 oz. citron
1 teaspoon nutmeg	1 cup currants
1 cup butter	1 cup seedless raisins

Crumble the yeast cake in the lukewarm water and stir until dissolved. Sift the flour with the spices. Cream the butter and then add the sugar, beating until smooth. Add the eggs, one at a time, beating until light after each addition. Add the sherry and brandy and mix thoroughly. Then add the citron, currants, and raisins. Add half the flour and stir until smooth; then add the yeast, stir again, add the remaining flour, and stir again until mixed. Turn into a greased, floured tube pan and let stand in a warm place until it rises—for about two hours. Bake at 350° F. for one and a half hours.

JULY 15

Saint Swithin's Day

We are entering now the period known as "dog days" and which in many places marks the beginning of the rainy season. We would therefore like to speak first of St. Swithin's as one of the "weather saints," for as the saying goes,

Saint Swithin's Day, if thou dost rain,
For forty days it will remain;
Saint Swithin's Day, if thou be fair,
For forty days 'twill rain nae mair.

Saint Swithin's connection with the weather, and particularly with the rain, doubtless comes from the legend that in his humility he asked to be buried outside his cathedral, where passers-by would step over his grave and raindrops from the eaves would fall upon it. He lived in the ninth century and was for a time one of the counselors of Egbert, a Saxon king. Later be became Bishop of Winchester, where great devotion to him long prevailed. Little else is known of him save that his feast is celebrated on the date when his relics were removed from the humble grave he had desired and placed, nearly a century after his death, in a new shrine built for him, where many miraculous cures took place.

And while we are on the subject of "weather saints," it might be pointed out that similar prophecies on certain days are made in various European countries although there is a difference of opinion as to the particular date in question. In France, for example, the feast of Saint Medard on June 8th, and the day of Saints Gervasius and Protasius, which falls on June 19th, have a similar character ascribed to them, as demonstrated by the verse:

S'il pleut le jour de Saint Médard,
Il pleut quarante jours plus tard;
S'il pleut le jour de Saint Gervais
et de Saint Protais,
Il pleut quarante jours après.

We have already spoken of Saint Medard on his feast day. We know little about Gervasius and Protasius other than that they were revered as the first martyrs of Milan, that they were the sons of another martyr, named Vitalis, and that they were put to death in Nero's time. Though they died in the first century, it is said that Saint Ambrose discovered their relics while digging the excavations for his cathedral in 386 A.D. and had them interred there.

Belgium has its rainy saint, namely Saint Godelième, of whom little is known other than that she was a holy woman in Flanders who was cruelly treated, and finally murdered, by her inhuman husband. Ever since her death in the eleventh century she has been venerated as a martyr in Belgium, and particularly in Ghent.

The Germans ascribe a similar character to the day of the Seven Sleepers of Ephesus, July 19th. The story of the persecution of these saints under Decius in 250 A.D. is too well known to be repeated here. In fact, they were so notable that the Greek and all other Eastern Churches list them in their catalogues of saints and even Mohammed introduced into his Koran a myth borrowed from them.

To return to Saint Swithin, besides the rain, his specialty is apples.

He blesses Bramley Seedlings
For dumplings or pie;
Blenheims will keep till Christmas
If lofted cool and dry;
And scarlet crabs for jelly
And Coxes ripe from Kent
Shall round an English belly
To apple-fat content,

says Elizabeth Sewell in a delightful poem published in *Duckett's Register*. And she ends:

High in the Heavenly Places
I see Saint Swithin stand.
His garments smell of apples
And rain-wet English land.

So in honor of Saint Swithin we may make

Apple Dowdy

Peel and quarter firm, tart apples and place them in a baking dish. Sprinkle light brown sugar over them, the amount depending upon the sweetness of the apples. Dust with a very little cinnamon, and grate nutmeg over the top. Dot generously with butter and pour over ½ cup of warm water. Cover the top with a rich biscuit dough, rolled about ¾ of an inch thick, slash a few holes to allow the steam to escape, and bake in a 300° F. oven for *three* hours. Serve with thick, unwhipped cream.

JULY 16

Feast of Our Lady of Mount Carmel

Celebration of the feast of Our Lady of Carmel goes back to the fourteenth century. Originally a feast of the Carmelites, it took its name from that order's first monastery on Mount Carmel in Syria, and it became in the eighteenth century a feast of the universal Church.

Devotion to Our Lady of Carmel is great in various European countries, and this title of the Blessed Virgin has given rise in Spain to such baptismal names as Carmen and Carmela and in Italy to Carmine and Carmelo. The Italians especially are devoted to Our Lady of Carmine. She has long been the patroness of Naples.

Often in the cities of the United States where Italian immigrants have arrived in large numbers during the years, one can see today, carried on as in the homeland, celebrations of this beloved feast. In the Italian section of New York City windows and balconies are everywhere decorated with red and green and white bunting and streamers. The streets are a sea of booths, and outside altars are constructed, sometimes two and three stories high. Among the gay crowds in the streets, carts are being pushed along laden with *Torrone* (nougat) and frosted cakes and candies of such bright colors that to the unaccustomed eye they suggest indigestion if not death. But evidently Our Lady of Carmine takes good care of her clients: there is a saying that no one will ever be taken ill on her day or as a result of its celebration.

Since she is reputed to heal ailments of all kinds, we find booths displaying replicas of various portions of the human anatomy, and their sale is brisk. Among the surging crowds we see people holding high in the air a waxen arm or leg to keep it from being broken. They are on their way to church to beg for the relief of some ailment or to place their wax offering before a shrine in thanksgiving for a cure. And somewhere in the long procession which crowns the celebration is the Virgin's statue so covered with money—some crackling new bills, others long saved and full of creases—that one can hardly see the image of the Lady in whose honor all this is done. The celebrations usually last for three or four days and, in New York before the last war, was regularly climaxed by a strange bit of pantomime. Stout wires were stretched from a fire escape on the fourth or fifth floor of one building to the fire escape of another across the street. At a given signal, shortly before midnight, a little girl gaudily attired in pink and furbished with a huge pair of waxen wings was propelled along the wire from each fire escape. As the two met in mid-air, they paused for a few minutes and then continued on their way to safety. The look of anxiety on the children's faces and that of admiration and ecstasy on the part of the onlookers was indeed something to behold.

In addition to *Torrone, Granita di Caffe* is a favorite sweet sold at tables and from carts along the streets.

Torrone (Nougat)

1 cup honey	½ lb. hazelnuts
2 egg whites	1 oz. candied orange peel
1 cup sugar	½ teaspoon grated lemon rind
2 tablespoons water	
1 lb. almonds	

Put the honey in the top of a double boiler over boiling water and stir for an hour—until the honey is carmelized. Beat the egg whites stiff and add slowly to the honey, mixing well. In a small saucepan boil the sugar and water until it also carmelizes, but do not stir. Slowly add the sugar to the honey and mix thoroughly. Cook for about five minutes more or until a little dropped into cold water hardens. Add nuts (the almonds having been blanched and the hazelnuts toasted in a hot oven for a few minutes), the candied peel, and the lemon rind. Mix quickly before the mixture hardens. Pour into well-oiled small loaf pans and after about twenty minutes cut into strips about two inches wide. Traditionally the top and bottom of the *Torrone* is covered with wafers which can be purchased at Italian confectionery stores. These wafers are called *Ostia.*

Granita di Caffe (Coffee Ice)

¾ cup sugar	½ cup lemon juice
2 cups warm water	2 cups strong coffee

Stir the sugar into the warm water until it is melted and add the lemon juice, stirring for about five minutes. Add the coffee, strain, place in a freezing tray, and freeze, stirring frequently, until it becomes a mush.

JULY 25

Feast of Saint James the Apostle

Tradition says that after the martyrdom of this son of Zebedee and Salome, the body of Saint James was placed in a rudderless boat with no steersman and allowed to float to sea. Under the guidance of angels it came to shore at Compostela in Spain. Later this town became the most famous place of pilgrimage in Christendom save for Jerusalem and Rome.

Saint James is the patron saint of Spain and of pilgrims in general. His symbol is the cockleshell, which has become the universal symbol of all pilgrims, and shellfish are especially connected with his feast. There is an old saying that he who eats oysters on Saint James' Day shall never lack for money. If a comfortable livelihood could really be so easily achieved, surely the lovers of the bivalve would be legion. But then the oyster beds would be emptied and the world would have to go to work again; so many circles that look pleasant in Utopia turn out to be vicious in our modern society.

In earlier days the street boys of London built grottoes of oyster and cockleshells on this day, and held out the largest one they could find to beg pence from passers-by. Since cockleshells are so particularly associated with this Apostle, we suggest as a most appropriate delicacy for this feast day *Coquilles Saint-Jacques.*

Coquilles Saint-Jacques
(Scallops or Cockles in the Shell)

- 12 scallops
- 4 oz. butter
- salt and pepper
- ½ lb. mushrooms
- 4 tablespoons sherry
- 2 tablespoons tomato purée
- 2 cups cream
- 4 egg yolks
- 3 sprigs chopped parsley
- lemon juice
- bread crumbs

Cut each scallop in two. Put them in a pan with the butter, salt and pepper to taste, and cook for about ten minutes. In another pan sauté the mushrooms in a little butter. When the mushrooms have cooked for about five minutes, add them with the sherry and the tomato purée to the scallops. Stir in the cream and the egg yolks but do not let the mixture boil. Add the chopped parsley and a little lemon juice. (If desired, add also a little finely chopped garlic.) Fill the mixture into scallop shells, cover with buttered bread crumbs, and run under the broiler for a very few minutes. (*Note:* Cockles and scallops are not of the same family. However, we suggest scallops here since they are much more easily procured. Incidentally, one of the French names for scallops is *pelerine,* meaning pilgrim.)

Saint James' feast was long pleasantly celebrated in rural England by the blessing of the new apple crop. The rector of the town was expected—and of course this was in the rationless seventeenth and eighteenth centuries—to distribute from his rectory "pyes" of mutton or beef to those who came to ask for them. The recipes are still at hand, and here is one high in favor in happier days.

Steak and Kidney Pie

1½ lbs. round steak
¾ lb. veal kidney
3 tablespoons butter
1½ cups chopped onion
3 cups stock
1 tablespoon Worcestershire sauce
salt and pepper
piecrust

Cut the steak into 1½-inch cubes and slice the kidneys. Melt the butter and brown the onion lightly. Add the steak and stir well until all sides are browned. Add the stock (or 3 cups boiling water with 3 bouillon cubes), cover, and allow to simmer for about one and a half hours. Then add the kidneys and cook an additional twenty minutes. Season with Worcestershire sauce, salt, and pepper. Place in a baking dish, cover with piecrust, making a slit for steam to escape, and bake at 450° F. for about twenty to twenty-five minutes or until crust is done.

JULY 26

Feast of Saint Anne

This is the day set aside by the Western Church to celebrate the feast of one who is not mentioned in the

Gospels but who is set down in tradition as well as in the hearts of thousands as Saint Anne, the mother of Mary.

She is especially beloved in France where, according to one ancient account, *la bonne Sainte Anne* was born. She is said to have gone from the land of Brittany to the land where she gave birth to Our Lady; and later, for love of her own country, she returned to Brittany to live, when her daughter was grown up and married to Joseph. All over France there are many churches in her honor and many harbor relics of Saint Anne.

The patroness of Brittany, a little saying sums up the feelings of every Breton about her: "*C'est notre mère à tous.*" Religious processions and other celebrations take place on her feast and, since the gastronomic specialties of Brittany are all sorts of fish and crustaceans, they are always served on her day.

Langouste à la Crème (Lobster with Cream)

1 boiled lobster
2 tablespoons butter
1 jigger sherry
2 tablespoons cream sauce
1 cup cream
2 egg yolks
1 tablespoon butter, melted
3 tablespoons cream

Boil a medium-sized lobster and allow it to cool. When cold, split it in two and dice all of the meat. Heat 2 tablespoons of butter and sauté the lobster meat in it for several minutes. Add the sherry, the cream sauce, and then the cup cream. Simmer gently for about ten minutes and then add the beaten egg yolks mixed with the remaining butter and cream. Mix all thoroughly and fill the lobster shells. Bake in a hot oven until lighty browned, or, while still hot, run under the broiler. (*Note:* Although the original recipe calls for crawfish, this is not easily nor always obtainable, and lobster may be substituted.)

France has carried its devotion to Saint Anne to the New World and in the little town of Beaupré in Canada she is held in especial reverence. Devotion to her goes back to the year 1650 when in the first house of the town was built a tiny altar in her honor. Eight years later a small chapel was erected to her, and it is told that she showed her appreciation by healing a crippled old man who had carried bricks for her building.

Today, on either side of the doors of the great Basilica of Saint Anne de Beaupré, piles of bandages and crutches are left by hundreds of her grateful clients. Pilgrims by thousands stream through the little town sometimes called "the Lourdes of Canada."

In Hungary Saint Anne's day is a great feast and is known as Mother's Day. It was formerly a holiday when the rich indulged in fine Anna balls, the peasants in folk dances and merrymaking of all kinds, and when the traditional Anna Fairs were held in towns and villages.

JULY 29

Feast of Saint Martha

Saint Martha, one of the best loved saints in the calendar, is called by the French *la travailleuse de Dieu*—the worker for God; this we know she was always and in more ways than one. The Italians know her as *l'albergatrice de Cristo*—the hostess of Christ.

She is the patron of cookery and of housewives. We all know the familiar story of how, as she was busied with preparing the dinner, her sister Mary sat at the feet of their Guest and listened to His words of love and wisdom. Martha, who was no doubt preparing a very special meal in His honor, needed help, and who, she reasoned, could better give it than Mary, sitting there with idle hands? Once the meal was served, she no doubt thought, there would be plenty of time to fold one's hands and listen to conversation—and perhaps her irritation came from the fact that she too wanted to hear the Words that were being spoken in the other room.

We are certain that every housewife, though she might prefer being a Mary, has a sneaking sympathy for Martha. For is it not very true that there are more Marthas than there are Marys in the world? And if there were not, please tell us who would feed everyone, including the Marys? There is something touching in the complete forgetfulness of Mary, her total absorption in unworldly things. But what if Martha had added herself to the company and listened too? Instead she remained with her task, and we are sure produced a good meal for that reason, so it is to her that housewives ought to turn.

In honor of her feast why should we not reproduce some of the ancient Jewish dishes, prepared in the same way as they were in Our Lord's day?

The Jews have a Hebrew expression about good food in general, but about Purim sweets in particular, *Tahm Gan Eden*, which means the taste, or flavor, of the Garden of Eden. One of the Purim sweets is the Poppy Seed Cooky.

Poppy Seed Cookies

- ½ cup milk
- 1 cup poppy seeds
- ½ cup butter
- ½ cup sugar
- 1½ cups flour
- 1 teaspoon baking powder
- 1 cup currants
- ¼ teaspoon cinnamon
- pinch of salt

Scald the milk, cool, and then soak the poppy seeds in it. Cream the butter and sugar together. Add the remaining ingredients, mixing well. Drop from a teaspoon on a greased cooky sheet. Bake at 350° F. for about twenty minutes—until lightly browned on the bottom. To brown the tops, run under the broiler for a few seconds, watching that they do not burn.

One of the traditional Jewish dishes always to be found at the Passover Seder is *Charoses*, a mixture of nuts and apples moistened with wine, to represent the morsel of sweetness to lighten the burden of unhappy memory.

Charoses

½ cup walnuts
½ cup almonds
1 cup grated apple
sweet red wine
1 tablespoon sugar
¼ teaspoon cinnamon

Chop the nuts and apple together or run them through the food chopper. Mix with sufficient wine to form a paste. Add sugar and cinnamon.

There is a tradition that after Martha and Mary lost their beloved Friend, they were driven, with their brother Lazarus, from their own country and were placed with other followers of Christ on a little vessel which bore them through stormy seas safely to Provence. There, the story goes, Lazarus became a bishop and was eventually martyred. Mary became a contemplative, shutting herself away on the heights of La Baume, and giving herself to penance and prayer. Martha, however, remained with the people in the valley, and is said to have founded the first convent for women at Aix. We are told that she bent the knee a hundred times a day at her devotions and as many times during the night. At last she, too, had time to pray.

For her day there is really no need of recipes since she is the patroness of all cookery. But here are three excellent hors d'oeuvre that hail from Provence.

Ratatouille

eggplant
zucchini
tomatoes
green peppers
2 cloves garlic
salt and pepper
olive oil

Take equal amounts of eggplant, zucchini, tomatoes, and peppers. Cut the eggplant and the zucchini into round slices as thick as a silver dollar. Peel the tomatoes and cut them into sections. Cut the peppers into ribbons, first removing the seeds, of course. Mix all together in an earthenware casserole. Finely chopped onions may be added but this is optional. But garlic is essential and two cloves of it should be used, whole (to be fished out later), chopped, or mashed. Sprinkle with salt and pepper and cover generously with olive oil. Cover the casserole and simmer gently for about three hours, taking the lid off during the last hour so that the vegetable liquid boils down to a syrup. Serve cold.

Poireaux à la Provençale (Leeks à la Provence)

3 lbs. leeks	12 black olives
3 tablespoons olive oil	juice of 1 lemon
salt and pepper	1 teaspoon chopped lemon peel
½ lb. tomatoes	

Clean the leeks thoroughly and chop into half-inch lengths. Put the oil in a shallow casserole and, when it is heated but not too hot, add the leeks, season with salt and pepper, and simmer for about ten minutes. Add the tomatoes cut in half, the olives which have been stoned, the juice of the lemon, and the lemon peel, and simmer for another fifteen minutes. Serve cold.

Provençal Salad

Mix equal amounts of shredded celery and chopped water cress, the grated peel of ½ orange, 3 sprigs of chopped parsley, 6 stoned black olives, chopped, and 2 sliced tomatoes. Make a dressing of one part lemon juice and two parts olive oil. Toss just before serving.

AUGUST 1

Lammas Day—
Feast of Saint Peter in Chains

So OFTEN in the course of centuries what was once a pagan festival became a Christian one, and various heathen observances were transplanted by early workers in the Christian vineyard and made to bear new fruit. Such a feast is Lammas Day, which replaced in early Britain the druidic feast of the Gule of August, marking the reaping of the first fruits of the year and particularly the earliest harvest of grain. Today scarcely observed at all, it was for many centuries a festival of importance on the Church calendar, and marked and still marks the feast of St. Peter in Chains. We are told this feast was instituted "to replace a harvest celebration of heathen origin," and in honor of the dedication in the fourth century of the Roman church of St. Peter Advincula on the Esquiline Hill where we may still find preserved small remnants of the chains that bound the Apostle in prison.

In Britain the Christian observance was called Lammas (Lamb-mass), some think from the custom of presenting a lamb to the church on this date in honor of St. Peter. It is more probable that the name is derived from the Anglo-Saxon *hlaf-mass* (loaf-mass), for a loaf made from the first ripened grain was the more usual offering. We incline to this second explanation, because the origin of the word *hlaf-diga* has always been one of our favorite bits of etymology. *Hlaf-diga* means loaf-giver and the dispenser of bread, hence the mistress of the home. This title was softened to our gentler word, lady, and we wonder if there could be a better definition than this for the term.

In suggesting a special dish for this day we go back to the early custom in the British Isles of placing the first sheaves of corn over the church doors on Lammas Day and of carrying in procession effigies of the Corn Spirit called "corn maidens."

Corn Bread

- ¾ cup flour
- 2 teaspoons baking powder
- 2 tablespoons sugar
- pinch of salt
- ¾ cup yellow corn meal
- 1 egg
- 3 tablespoons melted butter
- ¾ cup milk

Sift the flour, baking powder, sugar, and salt and add the corn meal. Beat the egg, butter, and milk. Pour the liquid into the dry mixture and combine rapidly. Butter an 8 x 8 inch pan and place in the oven until piping hot. Pour the batter into the hot pan and bake for about twenty-five minutes at 425° F.

AUGUST 6

Feast of the Transfiguration

The origin of this Christian festival has been attributed to Saint Gregory the Illuminator who flourished in Lower Armenia during the fourth century. He is said to have substituted it for a pagan feast of Aphrodite called *Vartavarh* (the flaming of the rose) and the old name was retained, in that region at least, to designate the Transfiguration, because "Christ opened his glory like a rose on Mount Thabor."

In Armenian villages the day is still celebrated with unusual ceremonies in the course of which peasants lead to the church a sheep with decorated horns, on each tip of which is placed a lighted candle. Flowers, fruit, and sheaves are also brought and laid before the altar. Following this ceremony a fair usually takes place; there are races and games, and a crown of roses is the customary prize. During the feasting that follows is likely to appear.

Pilaff

3 cups cracked wheat	6 cups stock
4 cups minced cooked lamb	½ cup melted butter
	pepper
salt	cinnamon

Soak the cracked wheat (cracked barley may be substituted) overnight. Drain the wheat, mix with the meat, and salt to taste. Place in a large kettle, add about half the stock (water and bouillon cubes may be used, allowing one cube for each cup of water), and heat slowly. Cook for about an hour, stirring almost constantly and adding stock as necessary. Serve in hot, deep plates, pour melted butter over each serving, and dust with pepper and cinnamon to taste.

The Feast of the Transfiguration was slower to be observed in the Western Church and is not mentioned until the ninth century. It was made universal by Rome on the day when Hunyady gained his victory over the Turks on August 6, 1456. It is now the titular feast of the Church of St. John Lateran, and on this day the Pope presses a bunch of ripe grapes into the chalice at Mass or uses new wine. Also in Rome raisins are blessed on the Feast of the Transfiguration, and the Greek and Russian Churches too conduct a special ceremony for blessing grapes and other fruits.

Since the grape is given so much prominence on this feast, we may give the following recipe:

Spiced Grape Jelly

8 lbs. Concord grapes
2 cups vinegar
2 sticks cinnamon
1 tablespoon whole cloves
sugar

Wash, remove from stems, and drain the grapes. Put half of them in a preserving kettle, add the vinegar, cinnamon, and cloves and then the rest of the grapes. Cook gently for about fifteen minutes or until soft. Strain through a jelly bag without pressing so that the juice remains clear. Take 1 cup of sugar for each cup of juice, boil to the proper consistency for jelly, pour into hot glasses and cover with ½ inch of paraffin.

AUGUST 10

Feast of Saint Lawrence

We have come to the day of one of the great martyrs of early Christian times, said to have been roasted to death on a gridiron and to have laughed and joked even as he underwent this torture. He was, according to the legends, a gay and likeable young man, kindly and charitable to all.

Some say that the Perseids, which appear on his feast in the heavens, are sparks from St. Lawrence's gridiron; others say they are his tears. We incline to the latter explanation, for despite his general good spirits, he was a man who sorrowed over the poor. He was a deacon and became the chief personage of the Christian community upon the martyrdom of Pope Sixtus II, having in his keeping the modest funds of the persecuted Church. Threatened with arrest, he begged for a day to put his affairs in order, and in due course, having distributed all in his possession among the poor, he appeared before the Roman magistrate followed by a crowd of beggars. When it was demanded that he turn over the treasure within his keeping, it is told he pointed to the outcasts and said,

"Behold the poor—they are the treasure of the Church." And the anger of the judge was so great that Lawrence was condemned to be burned to death over a slow fire.

Saint Lawrence's Day is celebrated all over Italy. In Florence, every home and restaurant serves

Lasagne

½ lb. ground beef
½ lb. ground pork
½ lb. ground veal
2 tablespoons olive oil
1 minced onion
1 clove garlic
1 teaspoon minced parsley
1 can tomato paste
1 cup tomatoes
2 cups water
salt and pepper
1 lb. lasagne
1 lb. Mozzarella cheese
¾ lb. ricotta cheese
grated Romano cheese

Brown the various meats in the oil, together with the onion, garlic, and parsley. Add the tomato paste (use the kind with basil in it), the tomatoes, and the water, season to taste with salt and pepper, and simmer from one and a half to two hours.

Immerse your lasagne, one piece at a time (to prevent sticking), in a large amount of salted, boiling water and cook for twenty minutes or until tender. Arrange a layer of lasagne in a baking dish, then sauce, then some Mozzarella, then some ricotta; continue this process until all the lasagne is used, ending up with ricotta on top. Sprinkle with grated Romano (or Parmesan) and bake in a 375° F. oven for about twenty minutes.

Although Lawrence died in Rome, he is said to have come from Spain, and is also greatly honored in that country. When Philip II won a battle over the French in 1557, he built in thanksgiving a monastery in honor of Saint Lawrence—and shaped it like a gridiron. This is the famous Escorial, so noted in Spanish architecture and history, and the burial place of the kings of Spain.

San Lorenzo's Day is honored all over the nation, and

he is the patron of many Spanish towns. At Huesca in Aragon his image is carried in a procession through the streets. In and out of the line of marching dignitaries, but without interfering with them in any way, weave the dancers of an intricate morris dance. (It is interesting to note that the word morris is a corruption of Moor.) When this procession is over, the statue of San Lorenzo is returned to his shrine and everyone attends a bull fight held in his honor. This is followed by one of the many-course Spanish meals which are the despair of foreign visitors, but they will surely like

Gazpacho (Cold Spanish Soup)

4 slices white bread
1 clove garlic
1 onion
1 cucumber
2 green peppers
salt
freshly ground pepper
dry mustard
1 tablespoon caraway seeds
olive oil
2 tablespoons vinegar
juice of ½ lemon
6 cups water
ice cubes

Remove the crusts from the bread, cut into cubes, and place in a soup tureen. Mince the garlic, slice the onion and cucumber, shred the peppers, and add to the bread in the tureen. Season with salt, freshly ground pepper, and a little dry mustard. Add the caraway seeds. Cover all generously with olive oil and mix thoroughly. Add the vinegar and lemon juice to the water and pour over the bread mixture. Put on ice for three or four hours. Serve in the tureen with ice cubes (about 6 or 8) floating in it.

In Paris there flourished for many centuries at the Halles, or market, the fair of St. Laurent, opening on the saint's feast and lasting for eight days thereafter. Here pleasure and commerce were combined in the most agreeable manner, and in our day as in that of Villon, the French visitor to the Halles is apt to demand *escargots*.

Escargots (Snails)

Snails are cooked for about half an hour in rapidly boiling salted water. Drain in a colander, remove the snails from the shells (which are reserved), and remove intestines. Then place the snails in another kettle, add a *bouquet garni* made of parsley, bay leaves, and thyme, a sliced onion, and a glass of cognac or other brandy. Cover with cold water, season with salt and pepper and, tightly covered, simmer for about three hours.

In the meantime scrub the shells and dry them thoroughly. Place a snail in each and cover the opening with garlic butter. Arrange the snails on a baking tin and place them in a medium-hot oven until the butter begins to run and the snails are heated through. The snails are served, ring-shaped, on a large platter without any garnish.

Garlic Butter for Snails

Pound 2 cloves of garlic in a mortar and remove any shreds (a garlic press is better if you have one) so that only the oil remains. Place ¼ pound butter in the mortar and work the garlic oil into it as well as you can. Then add a handful of parsley, chopped, a little salt, freshly ground pepper, and a pinch of nutmeg. Work all together until well incorporated.

Incidentally, Saint Lawrence is a patron of cooks and restaurant-keepers, a protector of vineyards, and invoked against fire and lumbago.

AUGUST 15

Assumption Day

The great feast of this month is that of the Assumption of the Blessed Virgin—the Day of the Great Lady, as it is called by a saint whose feast also comes in August:

Stephen, the first king of Hungary. In the Orthodox Church the feast is known as the Falling Asleep of the All Holy Mother of God.

This is not only Mary's greatest festival, but one of her oldest, for belief that she was taken up bodily into heaven after her death goes back to the early Christian ages, even though only recently has it been defined as a dogma of faith. "How shall Paradise not take her up who brought life to all mankind?" asks Saint Augustine, speaking of it as an accepted belief in his day.

Everywhere the day has its charming customs. In Eastern countries all women bearing the name of Mary, or a name derived from one of her attributes, keep open house in Our Lady's honor and welcome all who come.

In Poland the day is known as the Feast of Our Lady of Herbs, for the peasants take to church sweet-smelling bouquets of their finest blossoms mixed with the green of herbs. And Poles in America also honor the feast as that of Our Lady of Flowers; at church children sing hymns both in Polish and English, and later to the lively music of a polonaise the grown-ups swing into the dances of their motherland.

In many parts of Italy, the statue of Our Lady is carried in procession through the streets to the cathedral or church. And in Siena there takes place a noted race called the *Palio* (Standard) in honor of the Assumption of the Virgin. This race is held in the splendid public square of the city, shaped like a scallop shell and surrounded by ancient and beautiful buildings draped with banners for the occasion. Each ward or parish sends to the race a horse, which is first taken past the cathedral door to receive the bishop's blessing. The medieval costumes of the pages and grooms, of the captain and standard bearers, the furious race of the bareback riders around the stone-paved square, the crowds of onlookers from adjoining streets and balconies, make of this a memorable occasion. The winning parish or ward carries on a celebration after the race.

Scaloppine al Marsala

1½ lbs. veal cutlet	2 tablespoons butter
salt and pepper	½ cup marsala
flour	2 tablespoons stock

Have veal cut as thin as possible and then give it an additional pounding. Cut into serving pieces, salt and pepper, and dust lightly with flour. Melt the butter and brown the pieces quickly on both sides over a quick fire. When brown, add the Marsala and cook a few seconds more. Place on a warm platter, scrape the juices in the pan together with the stock and pour over the meat.

In Portugal the *Romeria*, as the festival held on the Assumption is called, is marked with the playing of a brass band and of drums and bagpipes. And the statues of Mary, Queen of the Angels, are crowned in the churches.

In Armenia there is the Blessing of the Grapes on the Sunday nearest the feast of the Assumption. Great trays of the fruit are brought into the churches, and after they are blessed each member of the congregation carries a bunch home. Feasts are held in the vineyards, and at this time the first grapes of the season are eaten.

In France August 15th is in general a day for parties and excursions into the country. At Quimper in Brittany, there is held the Feast of the Soul, dedicated to Mary as the great consoler. It is here considered a day for betrothals, when young men and women come to ask her blessing on their future. The image of the Virgin is placed at the church door during the day, and at night carried into the village square, later to be returned in procession to her shrine. Then to the light of bonfires and the music of bagpipes, the young people dance and make merry. A Quimper specialty is:

Crevettes à la Béchamel

(Shrimps with Béchamel Sauce)

Boil shrimps, about 1 pound, in heavily salted water for ten minutes. Remove from the shell and cut out the intestines. Heat in a béchamel sauce and serve in patty shells or in scallop shells.

Béchamel Sauce

- 2 tablespoons butter
- 1 tablespoon chopped onion
- ¼ cup flour
- 3 cups hot milk
- pinch of salt
- 4 peppercorns
- 2 sprigs parsley
- pinch of nutmeg (optional)

Melt the butter, add the onion, and cook until soft but not brown. Add the flour, mix thoroughly, and cook, stirring all the while, until the flour begins to turn golden. Add the milk, a cup at a time, stirring constantly. Add salt, peppercorns, parsley, and nutmeg (if desired). Cook for about twenty minutes, or until the consistency of heavy cream. Strain through a fine sieve.

AUGUST 16

Feast of Saint Roch

Saint Roch was born in France, but he is much venerated in other countries, especially in Italy where he spent a part of his life, and where San Rocco is highly honored in many towns and parishes. This saint lived in the thirteenth century, and came of a well-to-do family of Montpellier in southern France. Orphaned when young, he distributed his goods to the poor and donned the coarse habit of a pilgrim. His destination was Rome, and along the route he stopped at hospitals to care for the sick and to carry on other tasks of mercy. On his return he himself was stricken with the plague and lay dying of hunger and disease in a forest near Piacenza when there came into his life a faithful companion.

"It is Saint Roch and his dog" is an expression as proverbial as "Damon and Pythias" to designate two inseparable beings. In the forest Saint Roch was aided in his distress by a dog which each day brought him a piece of bread stolen with measured regularity from the table of his master. Becoming suspicious, this man followed the animal into the forest, found the dying pilgrim, became his friend and was led by him to a better life.

When Saint Roch returned to his native city after many years, he was so disfigured by his sufferings and mortifications that he was mistaken for a spy and thrown into a dungeon, where he died. Only after his death was he recognized, and a great devotion to him sprang up. Italians, at home and abroad, celebrate his feast. In Paris it was long a holy day of obligation. In Italy, Germany, and France, Saint Roch is considered the patron of surgeons, old-clothes dealers, wool carders, and of several other professions, and a protector against diseases of men and of animals.

Santo Roque is also honored in Spain, and here a special dish is named for him.

Saint Roch's Fingers

4 egg yolks
1/4 cup sugar
pinch of salt
2 cups scalded milk
1 tablespoon brandy
ladyfingers

Beat the egg yolks slightly and add the sugar and salt. Pour in the scalded milk slowly, stirring all the while, and place over a slow fire. Cook until mixture begins to thicken but do not allow it to boil. (It is safer to use a double boiler.) Strain and, when cool, flavor with 1 tablespoon of brandy. Arrange ladyfingers on the bottom and around the sides of a glass serving dish, pour in the custard, and serve when thoroughly chilled.

AUGUST 20

Feast of Saint Stephen of Hungary

This is the greatest Hungarian holiday, the feast of the first king and the patron saint of his country, converted from paganism to Christianity in the year 985. He made of Hungary a Christian nation and placed it under the patronage of the Mother of God. His feast was celebrated with special grandeur in Budapest, where until several years ago a most magnificent procession took place yearly, in which was carried aloft for public veneration the reliquary containing the incorrupt right hand of Saint Stephen.

Today these processions are only a memory in Hungary, although the day is celebrated by Hungarian exiles in other parts of the world. In happier times in Budapest, peasants from miles around poured into the city the night before his feast to await the procession. It started from the Chapel of the Royal Palace, where the relics were kept, and included hundreds of marching children, members of religious organizations, military leaders, and splendidly garbed officials of Church and State. Acolytes in white and red accompanied the last prelate bearing aloft the gold-encrusted reliquary. The line of march proceeded through the streets to the Matthias Church where Mass was celebrated, and returned afterwards to the Royal Chapel.

The festivities that followed often lasted the night through, and not until several days later had all the crowds departed. As usual in the old Hungary of better days, there was no lack of good food. Vegetables and fruit were plentiful, especially melons. And the people feasted on such dishes as *Paprikás Csirke* and *Gesztenye Krém.*

Paprikás Csirke (Paprika Chicken)

2 broilers
¼ lb. butter
3 onions, chopped
flour
salt
1 cup chicken bouillon
paprika
2 cups sour cream

Cut the broilers into serving pieces. Melt the butter in a large frying pan and sauté the onions until lightly browned. Add the chicken and continue cooking for about fifteen minutes. Turn the pieces from time to time so that they cook evenly. Remove chicken, add a little flour to thicken, and then the chicken bouillon, stirring until the sauce is smooth. Return the chicken to the pan and cook for another fifteen minutes or until tender. Remove pan from the fire and add paprika, anywhere from 1 to 2 teaspoonfuls until the desired sharpness and color is obtained. The sauce should be decidedly pink. Blend in the sour cream and return to stove but do not allow to boil once the cream has been added. Strain the sauce and pour over chicken. Serve with noodles or dumplings.

Gesztenye Krém (Chestnut Cream)

1½ lbs. chestnuts
1 cup water
1 cup sugar
1 cup cream, whipped
1 teaspoon vanilla
milk

Remove the outer and inner skins of the chestnuts and boil until soft with sufficient milk to cover. Pass through a sieve. Combine the sugar and water and cook for about ten minutes. Mix the chestnut purée and the sugar syrup and, when cool, add the vanilla and the whipped cream. Pile high on a serving dish and serve very cold.

AUGUST 24

Saint Bartholomew's Day

Of Saint Bartholomew it is said in *The Golden Legend* that he went to India to convert the pagans, as is told also of another Apostle, Saint Thomas. He was later martyred in Armenia, after telling the king who ordered him to adore the idols, "I shall fritter thy gods and thou shalt believe in mine." And at his words, the image of Baldach, the god, fell to the earth in its own temple. According to some, Bartholomew was beheaded, others tell that he was flayed alive and then crucified. On account of this latter legend, we often see him represented in art, as in the Last Judgment of Michelangelo, holding in his hand his own skin. Bartholomew's remains, the story continues, were tossed into a casket and set afloat and came ashore in Sicily, and after many centuries they were brought to Rome and are thought to be preserved in the Church of Saint Bartholomew-on-the-Island.

According to an Austrian legend, many years after his death Saint Bartholomew was seen walking through a field where a woman was working on his feast day. He chided her for this, but the woman was so upset to see the saint bleeding profusely and with his flayed skin over his shoulder, that she ran into the house and brought back some butter to anoint Saint Bartholomew's skin. Since that day Saint Bartholomew's butter is blessed on his feast in Austria.

In medieval times, Saint Bartholomew's Day was the occasion of a famous fair in England, first held in 1133. Henry the First granted a charter to hold this fair to a former minstrel who had become a monk and founded the Priory of Saint Bartholomew near London. It was opened on the eve of the feast and lasted for many days.

In later years, Barthelmy's Fair became a more raucous celebration, the center for strolling players to present their shows, and the rowdy merrymaking became so unrestrained that in the eighteenth century the fair was discontinued. But for many years it was a great occasion of fun and feasting. Carts and booths at the fair were heaped high with cakes and comfits; two specialties were gilt gingerbread and spiced nuts which the swains bought for their maids and the crofter for his wife and bairns.

White Gingerbread

1 lb. flour	¼ lb. butter
1 teaspoon ginger	6 oz. sugar
1 teaspoon soda	2 eggs

1⅓ cups milk

Sift the flour, ginger, and soda. Cream the butter with the sugar; add the eggs, then the sifted flour, and finally the milk. Let dough rest for a half an hour after mixing well, and bake at 350° F. for about thirty-five minutes.

AUGUST 25

Feast of Saint Louis of France

Against this great and good king, one of the principal patrons of France, one finds nowhere an unkind word uttered. His biographers emphasize his indifference to his own comfort, his deep and humble devotion to God and to the poor. He not only governed his nation in an admirable manner, but went as a crusader to the Holy Land with mind intent only on freeing the Holy Sepulcher from the hands of the infidel.

In the midst of wars, Louis was a lover of peace, and was often called upon to mediate between other Christian princes. Under the oak at Vincennes, he delivered wise and equitable judgments; his constant endeavor was not to appear imperious. Never impersonal about his charity, he fed beggars from his own table and daily gave meals to a hundred poor. He founded many hospitals and refuges, among them one for penitents and another for the blind.

Under his patronage, Robert de Sorbonne built in Paris the university which still bears his name. Louis appreciated and fostered learning, and there is the well-known story of an occasion when he invited Thomas Aquinas to dine at the palace. The huge philosopher sat in his place and said nothing at all, while about him the French conversation went on—"the most brilliant and noisy clatter in the world," says Chesterton, who tells the story with relish. Suddenly the table shook under the impact of a great fist. There was a startled silence as the company stared in amazement at Thomas. Unaware of them, and with another blow on the table, he said loudly, "And *that* will settle the Manichaeans!" Then it was that King Louis leaned over to one of his secretaries. "Take a note of this," he whispered, "and of anything more that he says. He might forget it and no doubt it is an important argument and a true one."

Louis was smitten by the plague and died in the East at the age of fifty-five, during the second crusade. He had been a good husband and father, devoted to his wife, Marguerite of Provence, and to his family of eleven children. Always at his side, to counsel him, had been his mother, Blanche of Castile, and on some occasions this great adviser had acted as his cook. For with her own hands, we are told, she was wont to prepare for Louis his favorite dish of lampreys, or eels. The recipe we have chosen is taken from *Le Cuisinier François* by Le Sieur de La Varenne, written in 1658 and, quite possibly, it was in this manner that good Saint Louis enjoyed his eel.

Pâté d'Anguilles (Eel Patty)

Cut the eel in rounds. Mix with it yolks of eggs, parsley, mushrooms, asparagus, soft roes, verjuice, or gooseberries if in season, and do not stint either butter, or salt, or pepper. Spread this on an undercrust and cover it with pastry. In order to hold it together, butter narrow bands of paper, and putting them around the pastry, bind them lightly on. Bake the pâté and, when it is cooked, mix the yolks of three eggs with a dash of verjuice and a little nutmeg; and when you are ready to serve, pour in your sauce into the pâté and mix it well. Open the pâté and serve with the crust cut in four.

SEPTEMBER 1

Feast of Saint Giles

THIS IS the feast of a saint as appealing as any in the calendar. Saint Giles, so identified with France, was, according to some, a Greek of the eighth century named Aegidius who passed over to Gaul and became a hermit, later founding a famous monastery under the Benedictine rule.

In his first retreat, his legend runs, he had little to eat, so God sent him a hind to feed him with her milk. One day the Frankish king of the land was out hunting, and coming across the hind, he prepared to shoot it with an arrow. But the animal ran to Giles for protection and the arrow meant for her pierced the leg of Giles. So, a cripple himself, he became the patron and protector of the lame. His relics are honored at Saint-Gilles in France, the town that sprang up around his abbey, where pilgrimages take place even today. He is also honored especially in other parts of France, in Germany, Poland, Spain, and the British Isles. Frequently depicted in art, his symbol is the hind.

In England, churches named for Saint Giles were built so that cripples could reach them easily, and he was also considered the chief patron of the poor. That in his name charity was granted the most miserable is shown from the custom that on their passage to Tyburn for execution, convicts were allowed to stop at St. Giles' Hospital where they were presented with a bowl of ale called Saint Giles' Bowl, "thereof to drink at their pleasure, as their last refreshing in this life." Once in Scotland during the seventeenth century his relics were stolen from a church and a great riot occurred.

In Spain the shepherds consider Saint Giles the protector of rams, and on his feast it was formerly the custom to wash the rams and color their wool a bright shade, tie lighted candles to their horns, and bring the animals down the mountain paths to the chapels and churches to have them blessed.

A similar custom prevails among the Basques. On September 1st, the shepherds come down from the Pyrenees, attired in their full costume, sheepskin coats and staves and crooks, to attend Mass with their best rams, in honor of Saint Giles. This is the beginning in the Basque country of a number of autumn festivals, marked by processions and dancing in the fields.

Soupe Basque

- ½ lb. dried beans
- 2 cups chopped onions
- 1 cup pumpkin pieces
- 1 cup chopped cabbage
- 1 clove garlic
- salt and pepper
- 8 cups stock

Soak the beans overnight, then rinse and drain. Brown the onion in a little bacon grease, then add the pumpkin, cabbage, beans, and garlic. Season with salt and pepper and add the stock. Simmer for about three hours in a covered soup kettle.

SEPTEMBER 24

Schwenkfelder Thanksgiving

Late in September is celebrated in the United States a day of Thanksgiving quite apart from the national holiday. It is held by the Schwenkfelders, a Protestant group who came from Germany in the year 1724 seeking religious freedom. In their wanderings they had met with persecution in many places and many of them had perished. Eventually those who survived, about forty families in all, came to settle in Pennsylvania. Worn and weary and poor, they reached Philadelphia on September 22nd, and two days later held a feast of thanksgiving. It was a very simple feast, consisting of bread and apple butter and water—nothing more.

Today the descendants of the Schwenkfelders are well able to hold a costlier celebration. But they still adhere to the old custom of a meal on this day, eaten after a thanksgiving service, of bread and apple butter and water.

Lattwaerrick (Apple Butter)

6 qts. cider
10 lbs. apples
8 cups sugar
2 tablespoons ground allspice
3 tablespoons cinnamon
2 tablespoons ground cloves

Boil the cider for about fifteen minutes or until reduced by half. Wash, peel, and cut the apples; drop into the boiling cider and cook until tender. Press the apples and juice through a sieve or food mill. Add the sugar and spices and cook to the consistency of a thick paste. The apple butter must be stirred frequently to prevent burning. (In olden times it was customary to put a handful of well-scrubbed marbles in the bottom of the pan. This was supposed to help prevent scorching, but stirring was still necessary.) Traditionally, the apple butter was stored in earthenware crocks in a cool cellar. This quantity can be filled into hot sterilized jars and then processed for about ten minutes. And as the Pennsylvania Dutch would say, "make tight shut."

SEPTEMBER 29

Michaelmas Day

To many, Saint Michael the Archangel, "Captain of the Heavenly Host," is best known as that dauntless spirit who vanquished his peer among the angels, Lucifer, once called "the Star of the Morning." Michael is a star of the love than conquers pride. Sometimes he is pictured as a winged angel in white robes, but oftener as the armed warrior on the errands of God, about his head a halo and under his foot the demon, prone and helpless. He was honored in Jewish tradition, and became the champion of Christian warriors as well, although in early ages he was also given the protection of the sick.

Of his early sanctuaries, the best known is Monte Gargano in Italy, where he appeared in the fifth or sixth century to the Lombards and insured their victory over the Greek Neapolitans.

In the Middle Ages Michael became in Normandy the patron of mariners. His shrines were built in high places, facing the sea, and Mont-Saint-Michel on its rock is the greatest example of devotion to him, a place of pilgrimage a thousand years ago as it still is today. In the early days much food was sold around the shrine—"bread and pasties, fruit and fish, birds, cakes, venizens," according to an old description. The fare is simpler today but a visitor to Mont-Saint-Michel will eat a famed and favorite dish:

Mère Poulard's Omelet

1/4 lb. butter	8 eggs

Melt the butter in a heavy frying pan (traditionally never used for any other purpose and never washed, merely being rubbed clean with salt after use) until it begins to froth and becomes a light golden brown. Beat the eggs with a fork slightly, just enough to mix the yolks and whites. Do not overbeat! Pour the eggs into the pan and cook gently, bringing the edges of the omelet as it cooks to the center of the pan, lifting the mass slightly so that the uncooked portion can run underneath. Increase the heat for about one minute, moving the pan about so that the omelet will slide in the pan. Invert on a platter and, when half is out of the pan, flip the pan quickly so as to cover with the remaining half. Do not salt as the quantity of butter used is sufficient to season the omelet properly. It is an old wives' tale that this omelet can only be properly prepared over a wood fire!

England long observed Michaelmas with many special ceremonies and customs. The Michaelmas daisy was named in the saint's honor, and village maidens in other days gathered crab apples on his feast. These were carried home and put into a loft, so arranged as to form the initials of their supposed lovers. The initials that were still perfect on *old* Michaelmas Day (October 11) were supposed to show where true love was. Another curious belief was that it was unlucky to gather blackberries on the feast of Saint Michael.

The outstanding and most persistent custom connected with Michaelmas was the eating of a goose at dinner. This seems to have originated with the practice of presenting a goose to the landlord when paying the rent. According to a sixteenth-century poet:

And when the tenants come to pay their quarter's rent,
They bring some fowl at Midsummer, a dish of fish in Lent,
At Christmas a capon, at Michaelmas a goose
And somewhat else at New-year's tide, for fear their
lease fly loose.

We read that Queen Elizabeth was eating her Michaelmas goose when she received the news of the defeat of the Spanish Armada. Obviously, this is apocryphal, for the "invincible" Armada was defeated in July and the news reached Elizabeth long before Michaelmas. But certainly the custom persisted in high places and low throughout Britain.

The Michaelmas goose was eaten in other places besides the British Isles, although in most countries of the Continent this custom was more apt to be connected with the celebration of Saint Martin's Day (November 11th). The Germans believed they could foretell the weather from the breastbones of the Michaelmas goose—a belief that traveled to America with immigrants of German stock, and which still exists today among the Pennsylvania Dutch.

To Roast a Goose

No doubt the very best way to cook a goose is the English way. The old recipes speak of roasting it before an open fire, and we may assume that the fat would then be in the fire and the goose flesh free of it. (However, they did have pans underneath to catch the drippings.) For modern cookery, the stuffed goose should be pricked all over; then put in the oven; after an hour drain off the fat, prick it again, and after a while again drain off the fat. Today there are still many too many who throw away the goose grease, and any housewife of ye olde dayes reading of this would surely recommend that those who do so should be hung high on Tyburn. In the olden days it was carefully kept and used for a variety of purposes. In fact, even in the United States oldsters will tell you what a wonderful relief was goose grease for chilblains in their own young days—an injury far more prevalent when children plowed through wet snow to school than today when they ride royally in busses. Roast in an uncovered pan at 325° F., allowing twenty-five minutes to the pound.

Potato and Sausage Stuffing

6 cups cubed potatoes
3 tablespoons chopped onion
3 tablespoons butter
¾ lb. sausage meat
3 tablespoons chopped parsley
1 teaspoon marjoram
salt and pepper

Peel and cube the potatoes and parboil for about five minutes. Saute the onion in the butter and add the potatoes, sausage meat, and parsley. Season with marjoram and pepper, and salt lightly because of the sausage meat. Apples may be substituted for the potatoes but in that case omit the marjoram.

Chestnut Dressing

6 cups chestnuts	salt and pepper
½ lb. melted butter	1 cup chopped celery
4 tablespoons chopped parsley	2 cups bread crumbs
	2 tablespoons grated onion

Shell, skin, and boil the chestnuts in salted water until tender. Mix with the remaining ingredients and, if the stuffing appears to be too dry, moisten with ½ cup heavy cream.

In Ireland, Michaelmas was one of the most important feasts of the year, and people prayed especially on this day for protection against sickness. A goose or a sheep or a pig was especially killed and eaten at Michaelmas at a feast of thanksgiving, connected by some with a miracle of Saint Patrick performed with the aid of Michael the Archangel. And the Irish made a Michaelmas Pie into which a ring was placed—its finder was supposed to have an early marriage.

In Scotland, Saint Michael's Bannock was made on his day, as well as a Saint Michael's Cake, that all guests, together with the family, must eat entirely before the night was over.

OCTOBER 4

Feast of Saint Francis of Assisi

From his early biographers we learn a charming incident in the life of the Little Poor Man of Assisi which deals with food even for this most abstemious of saints.

It was in the year 1212 that Saint Francis became acquainted with a young woman of the Roman nobility, Lady Jacoba di Settesoli, widow of the knight Gratiano Frangipani. The name Frangipani had been given the family because an ancestor had saved the Roman people from famine by giving them bread—hence the name *Frangens panem.*

Jacoba, a very devout woman and noted for her great generosity, often gave lodging to the Poverello when he came to Rome. So impressed was he with the energy and the capability of his friend that he called her "Brother Jacoba," by which title she passed to posterity. She not only saw that Francis' clothing was in decent order, but she served in her home a sweetmeat of which he was very fond. *Frangipane* it was called in later years—a concoction of almonds and sugar, for which the saint expressed perhaps the only compliment on cooking in his life.

Because Brother Jacoba was so good to him, Francis gave her a lamb which he had cherished and allowed to accompany him about, in honor, says Saint Bonaventure, of Our Lord Jesus Christ, the gentle Lamb of God. The lamb adopted Jacoba in the same way and "it would follow its mistress to church, lie down near her when she prayed, and return home with her. If Lady Jacoba overslept in the morning, the lamb would come to awaken her and would bleat in her ear to compel her to go to her devotions."

When he lay dying, Saint Francis thought of Brother Jacoba. "She would be too sad," he said to Brother Bernard, "to learn that I had quitted the world without warning her," and he dictated a letter, telling her the end of his life was near, that she was to set out as quickly as possible for Assisi to see him once more, and to bring with her a piece of haircloth as a shroud for his body and whatever else was necessary for his burial. "Bring me also," he ended, "I beg thee, some of those good things thou gavest me to eat in Rome when I was ill."

But the letter was barely finished and still unsent when the noise of horses was heard. Jacoba entered with her two sons and her servants, having been inspired to set out for Assisi from Rome. When one of the Brothers told Francis he had good news and before he could say more, Francis spoke. "God be praised. Let the door be opened, for the rule forbidding women to enter here is not for Brother Jacoba."

She had brought everything he needed—the veil for his face, the cushion for his head, the haircloth, the wax for the watching and funeral ceremonies. And she had brought also some of the almond sweetmeats he loved. He tried to eat them, but found he could take only a taste and he gave the rest to Brother Bernard.

Today we know *Frangipane* as a sweet almond cream flavored with red jasmine extract or a similar essence. It is used as a filling for cakes.

Frangipane Cream

2 eggs	pinch of salt
3 egg yolks	2 cups scalded milk
6 tablespoons sugar	1 teaspoon vanilla extract
12 tablespoons flour	6 stale macaroons

3 tablespoons sweet butter

Stir the eggs and egg yolks and add the sugar mixed with the flour and salt. Slowly stir in the scalded milk and continue stirring over a slow fire until the mixture thickens. Remove, add the vanilla extract, the macaroons which have been finely crushed, and the butter. Stir from time to time so that the cream is cold before using. (Red Jasmine extract is most difficult to come by, but should any reader be fortunate enough to procure some, 6 drops may be added.)

OCTOBER 25

Feast of Saints Crispin and Crispinian

This is the feast of two brothers, whose names are oddly alike. Both were bootmakers and cobblers. In France, their native land (though *The Golden Legend* tells us that they were Romans who had migrated to Soissons), many useful objects bear their name. A shoeshine kit is called a "Saint-Crispin"; an awl is "Saint Crispin's lance"; and if your shoes are too tight, you are "in Saint Crispin's prison."

Because of their refusal to sacrifice to idols, Saint Crispin and Saint Crispinian were pierced with shoemaker's awls and suffered other tortures. They were in popular veneration throughout the Middle Ages, and we read in Shakespeare's *Henry the Fifth:*

This day is call'd the feast of Crispian:
He that outlives this day, and comes safe home,
Will stand a tip-toe when this day is nam'd,
And rouse him at the name of Crispian.

For many years there was a special Mass for the cobblers of France on this feast and it was followed by a huge banquet. Legend says the first celebration of this Mass so pleased the saints that they allowed cobblers to have as reward a little preview of heaven.

In England, the same custom of a special feast on Saint Crispin's day was observed by the shoemakers. Afterwards they burned torches on the sand, probably as substitutes for the altar lights provided by the shoemakers' guild in pre-Reformation times for their chantry chapel.

Just as, some months back, on Saint Anthony's Day we allowed a recipe having as its title a pun, so we give you another for the day of the shoemaking saints.

Fruit Cobbler

3 cups fruit
½ cup sugar or more
1 tablespoon flour or
1 egg
biscuit dough

A cobbler may be made with the fruit *on top* of a biscuit dough or with fruit *under* the dough. Prepare the fruit and add sugar (the amount will vary with the sweetness of the fruit) mixed with flour or with a well-beaten egg. Make a rich biscuit dough (or use prepared mix) and place in the bottom of a greased baking tin; cover with fruit dotted with bits of butter and bake at 425° F. for about half an hour. Or, cover the fruit with the dough and brush the dough with a little milk or the beaten yolk of an egg diluted with a little water. Apples, peaches, plums, or other fruits may be used.

OCTOBER 28

Feast of Saints Simon and Jude

Not very much is known of either of these Apostles, except that Simon was called "the Zealous," and Jude was the brother of James the Less, and that they preached and were martyred in Persia.

Over the years great devotion has grown up around Saint Jude as the Saint of the impossible. As prayers to Saint Anthony restore lost articles, so prayers to Saint Jude restore or revivify the most difficult of spiritual causes for persons, or groups, or nations. Saint Jude has proved a powerful patron in more than one instance, for example in the case of the City of St. Jude in Alabama, founded to aid materially and spiritually the Negro race, and which has well fulfilled that mission. Saint Jude might make a fine patron for the United Nations, over endowed with material patrons, but sadly lacking in those of the spirit.

Regarding popular celebration of the feast of Saint Simon and Saint Jude, there has arisen some confusion through the centuries. In Italy a *foletto*, which translated, means holy goblin, was often confused with Saint Simon because of a similarity in names, and Jude was confused in people's minds with Judas. Another reason for the confusion is that the feast of these saints comes so close to All Hallow's Eve that it partakes a little of its traditions.

From the old association with goblins and witches and feasts of the dead, there has come down to us a cake often eaten in Scotland and England in honor of Simon and Jude. In Scotland, it is known as a Dirge Cake, in England as a Soul Cake, and we give the recipe on November 2nd, the feast of All Souls.

OCTOBER 31

All Hallows' Eve

A very ancient celebration is this the Eve of All Saints. In pre-Christian eras it was a day when the Druids gathered within a ring of stone and chanted runes. The Romans celebrated it with an autumn feast to Pomona, goddess of orchards.

In the calendar of the Church this is a fast day, but, especially in Ireland, many interesting dishes have been evolved to tide one over to the next day's feast of All Saints. Fast days often seem to inspire cooks to concoct palatable foods of a vegetarian nature. Of these the counties all have their favorites, most of them based on the potato, that basic commodity from the Irish fields. But no matter what the food, there is always placed in the dish a wedding ring wrapped in grease-proof paper, and this is said to decide the future of the person finding it.

Tyrone, Cavan, and other counties indulge in boxty dishes and also in many verses about them. One runs:

Boxty on the griddle,
Boxty on the pan,
The wee one in the middle
It is for Mary Anne.

Boxty on the griddle,
Boxty on the pan—
If you don't eat boxty,
You'll never get your man.

And another:

Two rounds of boxty baked on the pan,
Each one came in got a cake in her han';
Butter on the one side,
Gravy on t'other
Sure them that gave me boxty
Were better than my mother.

These boxty dishes include boxty dumplings and boxty bread and boxty pancakes (for the latter *see* Shrove Tuesday).

Boxty Bread

1 lb. raw potatoes	salt
1 lb. cooked potatoes	flour

Wash and peel the raw potatoes and grate them onto a piece of cheesecloth. Then squeeze them out, catching the liquid in a dish which must be allowed to stand so that the potato starch may settle. Mash the cooked potatoes over the raw, and season with salt. Pour off the potato liquid carefully; then scrape up the potato starch at the bottom of the dish and add to the potato mixture. Work in enough flour to make a good dough and knead for a few minutes; then roll out, cut into cakes, and bake on a hot griddle.

Boxty Dumplings

Use the same ingredients and follow the same procedure as for Boxty Bread. When the dough has been kneaded, instead of rolling it out, form into small balls the size of an egg, drop them into boiling salted water and cook them for forty-five minutes. Serve with a sweet sauce.

The same counties feature on Halloween Potato Pudding and Colcannon (*see* Saint Patrick's Day).

In Scotland a special cake is made, and charms wrapped in paper are stirred in before it is baked. These are the usual ring, button, thimble, and coin, with the addition of a horseshoe for good luck, a swastika for happiness, and a wishbone for the heart's desire.

In England, as also in the United States, it is a night for feasting before an open fire, on cider and nuts and apples, and was formerly known as Nut Crack Night.

Far back in history runs the list of games played on that night, many of them still popular, such as bobbing for apples in a tub of water, or trying to take a bite from one swinging on a cord, or that slightly more dangerous but fascinating sport of snapdragon, in which raisins were placed in a bowl of brandy and the liquid set on fire, the point of the game being to extract the raisins without burning oneself—surely a better game to win than to lose.

Although Halloween is the eve of a solemn church festival, its celebration has always been associated with witches and hobgoblins and ghosts; in the past it was at times an occasion for the practice of sorcery and incantations, and even of cruelty. Today it is a night of fun, which even at its worst seems to consist in the carrying away of gates or porch furniture. We have all seen the children, dressed in grotesque ways, who go about asking for candy and pennies. Familiar is the sight of the small boy coming home with a bag full of edibles—candies, cakes, nuts, gum, enough for several meals—and a good stack of pennies.

Grown-ups, whose duty for the evening seems to be to provide the handout, might spend their own evening by making it a Nut Crack Night. Sitting before a bright hearth fire, they can feast on the appropriate foods of the night and of the season—cider and apples and nuts.

NOVEMBER 1

All Saints' Day

THIS DAY, formerly known in England as All Hallows and in France called *Toussaint*, honors, as its name implies, all the saints canonized and uncanonized, known and unknown. Long ago the church bells rang for most of the night before All Saints' Day to praise the saints "risen in their glory." Everywhere patronal and family saints are especially remembered. It is a feast to give them praise rather than to ask favors of them, a day for praising them to God rather than asking them to remember the living to Him.

The observance of this feast merges into the next, which is All Souls' Day, so that by evening it has become the eve of the day of the dead. On All Souls' Eve the graves in Hungary are lighted with candles and decorated with flowers. Indeed, the custom of visiting the cemeteries and adorning the graves of relatives and friends with wreaths and bouquets prevails in most Latin and Central European countries.

In Czechoslovakia there is an old tradition of eating special cakes on All Souls' Eve, and of drinking cold milk "to cool the souls in Purgatory." In Belgium also a particular variety of cakes is baked, and it is an old superstition that "the more one eats of them the more souls will be saved from Purgatory."

In many old English towns, maids still go "souling" on All Souls' Eve, that is, singing for cakes, and one hears such ancient ballads as:

Soul! soul! for a soul-cake!
I pray, good misses a soul-cake—
An apple or pear, a plum or a cherry,
Any good thing to make us merry,
One for Peter, two for Paul,
Three for Him who made us all.

Soul Cakes

1 yeast cake	2 cups milk
½ cup sugar	6 cups flour
¼ cup lukewarm water	1 teaspoon salt
¼ lb. butter	3 teaspoons cinnamon

Dissolve the yeast cake with 1 teaspoon of sugar in the lukewarm water and let it stand in a warm place. Cream the butter with the sugar. Add the milk which has been scalded and slightly cooled and then add the yeast. Sift the flour with the salt and cinnamon and add to the mixture, kneading for a few minutes. Place in a bowl and allow it to rise in a warm place to double its bulk. Shape the dough into round buns and bake at 375° F. for about thirty minutes or until lightly browned. Originally, these cakes were shaped like men and women and were given raisins or currants for eyes.

NOVEMBER 2

All Souls' Day

After the feast in honor of the saints in heaven, comes the day of praying for the dead, particularly for members of the family, so "that they may quickly attain to the fellowship of the heavenly citizens."

As we have said, many of the observances of this day take place on the eve. In the Old World lights were set in windows to guide the departed back to their homes, and food was placed beside a candle or lighted lamp on the table to await them. In Brittany, where belief in the supernatural is intensified on this night, the people, dressed appropriately in black, hurry home after vespers to talk together about the departed, speaking of them in low tones as if at a funeral. On the table with the best cloth are placed plates of bread and cheese and mugs of cider for the refreshment of the departed ones. As the living sit whispering together, they hear, or seem to hear, in creaking floorboard and empty benches about the table the movements of the ghosts who have come to rest that night in their former home. And knowing that the saddest of all are the homeless dead who roam about the countryside on this one night of the year permitted them on earth, it is a custom of Celtic people to set food and drink on doorstep and window sill, so that homeless spirits too may have a share.

In Italy, and especially in Sicily, good children who have prayed for the dead through the year are rewarded by having the *morti* leave gifts, sometimes cakes, none the less welcome because they have been made by the hands of mundane bakers. Especially good are these *Fave dei Morti*, and as fine a reward for a pious child as was the *Pretolium* or pretzel of the Middle Ages.

Fave dei Morti (Beans of the Dead)

¼ lb. almonds — **butter, size of a walnut**
¼ lb. sugar — **1 teaspoon cinnamon**
2 tablespoons flour — **1 egg**
½ lemon peel, grated

Pound some of the almonds (unblanched) with some of the sugar in a mortar, and then rub through a sieve. Continue this process until all of the almonds and sugar have been used. Any of the mixture remaining in the sieve should be pounded again until it is fine enough to pass through the sieve. Work this paste with the flour, butter, cinnamon, egg, and lemon peel until the whole is quite

smooth. When done, roll into long thin rolls; divide into small pieces and shape them to resemble a broad bean. Bake on a greased tin at 350° F. for about twenty minutes or until light brown. Though soft at first they will harden when cold.

In Poland on All Souls' Day vespers are sometimes sung in the churchyards, and alms are given to the poor who in return are expected to offer prayers and petitions for the dead of the donor's family. Lighted candles are placed on the graves to drive away the bad angel so that "the Lord may count on that night the number of souls belonging to Him."

In Spain every theater gives a performance of the famous play *Don Juan Tenorio* and thrills anew to the drama of the wicked lover who is dragged to hell by the ghost of the fair damsel to whom Don Juan proved unfaithful. The *Dia de Muertos* is an occasion so important in Mexico that its observance lasts for several days. Several days before, on October 30th, the souls of dead children are said to revisit their homes and spend the night. They are welcomed with flowers and food in gourds, as many gourds as there are *angelitos*—souls of dead children—expected. And in the doorway of homes are placed chocolates and cakes and a lighted candle for those children who have no one to remember them.

On the Day of the Dead, Mexican crowds stream into the cemeteries long before daybreak, bearing flowers, candles, and food. Breads, candies, and cakes have been made in the form of grinning skulls with eyes of shining purple paper, of little chocolate hearses and coffins and funeral wreaths. With picnic gaïety the families group about the graves in the cemeteries, everyone laughing and enjoying the fine fiesta and sharing the food they have brought. And as in Spain, in the evening the whole village repairs to see the perennial drama of the faithless Don Juan and his luckless lady.

Pan de Muertos (Bread of the Dead)

1 yeast cake	2 cups sugar
¼ cup lukewarm water	6 eggs
5 cups flour	⅓ cup orange blossom water
1 teaspoon salt	⅓ cup milk
1 cup butter	

¼ cup anisette

Dissolve the yeast in the lukewarm water and let it stand in a warm place. Sift the flour with the salt. Taking about half the flour, add the yeast, mix well, and allow to rise in a greased bowl in a warm place until double in bulk. Cream the butter with the sugar; add the egg yolks and the orange blossom water. Then add the remaining flour, the milk and anisette. Mix well and knead for a few minutes. Then add the egg whites, one at a time, kneading after each addition. Finally add the fermented dough and beat and knead until thoroughly mixed. Allow it to rise in a greased bowl in a warm place until double in bulk. Knead once more and divide into two portions. Remove a bit of the dough from each portion, enough to form two "bones." Shape the dough into round loaves and moisten the tops with water. Place the "bones" in the shape of a cross on each loaf and bake at 375° F. for about fifty minutes or until done. The loaves are usually covered with a light sugar glaze when baked.

NOVEMBER 3

Feast of Saint Hubert

Late in the eighth century, so runs the story, a hunter named Hubert, neither better nor worse than he should have been, was tracking a stag through the forest of the Ardennes. As he readied himself to shoot the animal with his arrow, he was startled when the stag turned suddenly in its flight, and he saw between its antlers a luminous cross. This experience caused Hubert to change his way of life, and he never hunted again. Yet only a few centuries later he was known as the patron of hunters, and is a saint greatly honored in France and Belgium.

Saint Hubert lived a full life. He became bishop of Tongres and traveled through his huge diocese on horseback and by boat, preaching and building churches to the glory of God. He was the friend of the great of his day—Pepin of Heristal and Charles Martel among them—and also of the poor. In particular his heart went out to prisoners, and he would secretly place food for them before their dungeon windows. As he died he said to those about him, "Stretch the pallium over my mouth for I am now going to give back to God the soul I received from Him."

In parts of France and Belgium there has long been a custom of holding stag hunts on Saint Hubert's Day, and the hunters gather before the chase for Mass and the blessing of men and horses and dogs. After the hunt is over, those taking part gather for a bountiful breakfast consisting of fish, meat, salad, cheese, and dessert. Naturally the meat is venison of some sort, and the salad may well be one of dandelion greens.

Venaison Rôti (Roast Venison)

If the venison is young, it does not need marinating; otherwise marinate several hours or even overnight. For the marinade use 1 pint of vinegar, 1 pint of red wine, several bay leaves, 4 shallots, 2 sliced carrots, 1 lemon cut into thin slices, some freshly ground pepper, and a handful of juniper berries. Carefully remove the skin from a loin of venison without tearing the meat and wipe it with a damp cloth. Lard the loin symmetrically with bacon (*not* larding pork). Dust with salt and pepper, cover liberally with butter, and roast in a hot oven for one hour, basting almost continuously with the butter in the pan and 2 cups of sour cream. Remove the meat to a hot platter; carefully stir 1 tablespoon of flour into the pan, then add a cup of hot stock, cook for several minutes, and strain through a fine sieve. (Though not orthodox, a leg of lamb may be substituted but in that case marinate for several days.)

Pissenlit au Lard **(Dandelion Greens with Bacon)**

Wash the dandelion greens carefully to remove all grit and dry thoroughly in a salad basket. Cut up ¼ pound of lean bacon into dice and fry over a slow fire until very crisp. Add 3 tablespoons of tarragon vinegar to the bacon grease and season lightly with salt and freshly ground pepper. Pour, while hot, over the greens, mix well, and serve at once.

NOVEMBER 11

Feast of Saint Martin of Tours

The most common form of charity—and of hospitality—is to offer food; Saint Martin chose instead to give away his cloak. We most ordinarily think of him as the young soldier, cutting his cloak in two with his sword to give a part to the shivering beggar he met upon his way. We may think of him also when he became a Christian and a priest, proudly writing to his mother to beg her to become his first convert. She was the first of many he made, for he journeyed for many years about Gaul, preaching and baptizing, and throwing about all, and especially about the poor, his cloak of pity and love.

Martin became the bishop of Tours and there founded a monastery, dying in his see city, where his tomb has been a place of pious pilgrimage for over sixteen hundred years.

An interesting footnote to history is the story of what became of the other half of Martin's famous cloak. For many years it was carried into battle by the Frankish kings. We are told that it was then lost for a long time but eventually found again, and it is shown to visitors to Tours today, in a little chapel not far from the cathedral where rest Saint Martin's bones. And *The Golden Legend* tells us further that the place where Martin's cloak was kept was known as the place of the cloak, or cape (*cappella*); hence the origin of the modern word chapel.

Saint Martin is known as the patron of Saint Martin's summer, of swallows, and of winegrowers (and some say he is the protector of drunkards as well). His feast comes at that time in autumn when the new wines are tasted, when cattle are killed for the winter's food, and when geese are at their prime.

On the Continent the goose is the chief dish of the Martinmas feast, although, as we have seen, it was sacrificed in England earlier in the year, at Michaelmas. Even so there is an English adage that if you have roast goose for Martinmas, you must ask Saint Martin to dine with you or you won't get one next year. And to ask Saint Martin to dine means that you must share your goose with someone who has none, as Martin did his cloak.

In Germanic countries on Saint Martin's day, goose is eaten with sauerkraut. In Sweden the bird is stuffed with apples and prunes, though the fruit is usually discarded and is merely used to flavor the bird. The meal is begun with blood soup, made from the wings, neck, heart, liver, and blood of the goose and flavored with ginger, pepper, vinegar, sugar, and wine! Cinnamon Apples are the accompaniment for the Swedish goose.

Cinnamon Apples

Wash and core 6 apples of the same size but do not peel them. Half cover with boiling water and, when the apples are tender, remove and peel them. To the water in which they were cooked, add 1 cup of sugar and 1 teaspoon of cinnamon. Bring to the boil and reduce by half. Place the apples back in this syrup, spooning the juice over them until they are thoroughly reheated, and serve.

The famous goose dish of France, made especially in Alsace, is *Pâté de Foie Gras*.

Pâté de Foie Gras

Take 2 fine goose livers and with a sharp knife remove all of the skin and as much of the fiber as you can. Cut the livers into pieces. Line a small baking dish (it should have a cover) with thin slices of salt pork, covering both sides and bottom. Place the pieces of liver in the dish, adding small pieces of truffles (using about ½ pound in all) as you go along. Dust each layer with a little salt and pepper, and press down on each layer as you complete it. Pour over the top 2 tablespoons of the best cognac. Do not use any other spices. As an old French recipe says, *"Le sel et le poivre sont là uniquement pour corriger la fadeur du foie, dont le goût délicat ne doit se marier qu'au parfum de la truffle et à l'arome à peine définissable fourni par le cognac"* (The salt and pepper serve the unique purpose of correcting the blandness of the liver; its delicate flavor should only be married to the perfume of the truffle and the almost imperceptible aroma of the cognac). Place another slice of pork (all the pork used should be lean) on top, cover the dish, seal with a paste made of flour and water, and bake in a medium oven for an hour and a quarter. The baking dish should be set in another of hot water which should not be allowed to boil; as it evaporates, add more hot water.

When the pâté is done, take from the oven, remove the cover, and tap for several minutes with a spoon so that the grease in the dish begins to rise to the surface. Place a small plate directly on top of the pâté and, on this place a heavy weight, and allow it to stand for twelve hours. The grease will continue to come to the top, seep over the edges of the dish, or may be removed with a teaspoon. Smooth the top. Refrigerate and do not use for forty-eight hours. If the pâté is to be kept for any length of time, cover it with a layer of goose grease.

NOVEMBER 23

Feast of Saint Clement

Saint Clement, who became the fourth of the popes, is said to have been ordained by Saint Peter himself. To him has been attributed the literary work known as the *Clementines*, a long account which some have called the first Christian novel; it deals with the magician Simon Magus, with holy men and women, and with demons; of the latter it warns that the man who is greedy may swallow a demon with his food which will hide in his body forever after.

According to one legend, in fleeing from his persecutors Saint Clement suffered so much from blistered feet that he put wool in his sandals. This "felted" the wool and when he reached Rome and safety, he turned the accidental discovery to use and created the felt industry! Later martyred, his body was cast into the sea and ever afterward on the anniversary of his death, says the legend, the sea withdraws at that spot and reveals a little marble shrine where rest his remains.

In England Saint Clement is the patron saint of blacksmiths. It was the custom in former times for one of their number, in a great-coat and mask and long white beard, to be carried through the streets on the shoulders of his mates. One companion strode along beside him with a huge wooden anvil, and another, as if to protect him, carried a great wooden sledge. From his perch the "saint" made a speech beginning:

Gentlemen all, attention give
And wish Saint Clement long to live.

The feast of Saint Clement is still observed in the dockyards of London. Masters of the trade give a dinner to their workmen and apprentices which features a Wayz Goose, which is not a goose at all but a leg of pork stuffed with sage and onions.

Wayz-Goose (Stuffed Leg of Pork)

1 leg of pork	2 tablespoons parsley
1 cup bread crumbs	¼ teaspoon salt
¼ cup chopped celery	⅛ teaspoon paprika
½ cup chopped onions	1 teaspoon sage

milk

Prepare a stuffing of all of the above ingredients, adding enough milk to make a not too moist mixture. Have the butcher bone the leg (or use the lower half of the foreleg, called a picnic roast) and stuff the cavity, sewing it up with coarse thread. Roast in a 350° F. oven allowing thirty-five minutes to the pound.

Thanksgiving Day

Most of the feast days celebrated in the United States were brought to our country with the traditions of older lands. But of the festivals which belong entirely to us, one is Thanksgiving.

In 1620 when the *Mayflower* Pilgrims left their ship at Plymouth, they hastened first of all to give thanks to God for their preservation from the perils of the sea. Then they set to work to build a few houses and to sow wheat and barley and peas, helped in their task by friendly Indians who taught them how to use the native fruits and vegetables, the venison and wild fowl, and the many varieties of fish and shellfish which abounded in the coastal waters. One year later, after incredible hardships and the death of many of their number, the Pilgrims again gave thanks, this time for the harvest they had planted and which God had blessed for them.

This idea of giving thanks to God when the harvest is in is, of course, a very ancient custom. Moses commanded the Hebrews to celebrate a harvest festival, and it is still known as Succoth, or the Ingathering, and still celebrated. There were festivals in ancient Greece in honor of Demeter, goddess of the fields, and of Ceres in ancient Rome. The English Harvest Home is also very old.

But all these celebrated plenty, the plenty of years, and the result of years of cultivation of the land. Here in America, settled only briefly on an inhospitable coast and with but a single year of growth behind them, the Pilgrims gave thanks not for the old but for the new, not for the plenty of centuries but for the hard-earned, scanty yield of one year in a strange land.

The first Thanksgiving feast did not lack for guests; in fact, there were many more than the hosts had expected. Massasoit, the Indian chief who had shown much interest in the struggling band from overseas, was invited to the feast and told to bring some of his braves. He appeared accompanied by ninety warriors! The hosts welcomed them as hosts should, even though the unexpected number of guests cut deeply into their supplies laid aside for the coming winter.

The Indians brought gifts for the feast—five deer, quantities of lobsters and eels and wild turkeys. We are told there were very few to prepare this feast for one hundred and forty men. Five women and a few young girls were all that remained of the women who had come on the *Mayflower*, and this small band prepared the food for three days of feasting.

Among the dishes was one which the Indians had taught the English women to make, called in the Indian tongue *sauquetash*, from which comes the modern succotash. But the Indian dish was very different from what we understand by that name today. It was more like a soup and an old recipe tells us that it contained two fowl and, in a separate kettle, one-half pound of lean pork and two quarts of white beans. To the kettle containing the fowl were added pieces of corned beef, a turnip, six potatoes. When the meat was tender, it was removed and the two "waters" mixed together. Then four quarts of hulled corn were boiled till tender and added to the soup and the meat of one fowl cut up. The other fowl was served as a separate course with the corned beef and the pork.

There were even desserts at the feast—dried gooseberries and cherries and cranberries, cured by the Indian method. These berries were cooked in "dough cases"—no doubt the Pilgrim equivalent of pies. There was Indian pudding, made of corn meal and molasses boiled in a bag, and here is a modern version.

Indian Pudding

4 cups milk	½ teaspoon ginger
⅓ cup corn meal	½ teaspoon cinnamon
1 cup dark molasses	1 egg
¼ cup butter	½ cup raisins (optional)
1 teaspoon salt	1 cup milk (optional)

Boil the milk in the top of a double boiler. Stir in the corn meal and cook for about twenty minutes over boiling water. Then add the molasses and cook for another five minutes. Remove from the fire and add the butter, salt, spices, the egg beaten, and the raisins if used. Pour into a greased baking dish and bake at 300° F. for two hours. If you would have a soft center, pour the milk over the top. Serve with hard sauce or cream, though it is a New England custom to serve the pudding with vanilla ice cream.

And the Indians gave the white children their first taste of popcorn which they had made into balls with maple syrup.

In later years these feasts grew less rugged and more varied. A letter of 1779 tells of the Thanksgiving feast of that year in a well-to-do home—venison at one end of the long table, at the other chines of pork and roasted turkeys, and set between them pigeon pasties. And that year this household had "sellery" for the first time. There are mentioned also two oranges on the table, a very unusual fruit for that day in New England, and these were given to the two grandmothers of the family.

In 1789 the Congress of the United States suggested making legal a day of thanksgiving for signal favors from Almighty God, who had afforded the nation an opportunity "peaceably to establish a constitution of government for their safety and happiness." President Washington liked the idea and issued a proclamation to this effect. But after his death this special action was allowed to lapse, although the private custom of celebrating Thanksgiving remained popular.

Some sixty years later Mrs. Josepha Hale began campaigning to revive the custom of a national Thanksgiving. In 1846, she became editor of *Godey's Lady's Book* and used the pages of her famous magazine to foster this purpose. She argued not only with words but with recipes, some of which seem very heavy argument—she suggested "ham soaked in cider for three weeks, stuffed with sweet potatoes and baked in maple syrup," a prescription of rather overwhelming caloric strength.

Even the Civil War did not stop her efforts, and somehow she prevailed, for in 1863, in the very midst of the conflict, President Lincoln issued the first National Thanksgiving Proclamation since that of Washington, inviting all his fellow citizens, "and those also at sea and those who are sojourning in foreign lands," to set apart and observe the day "as a day of thanksgiving and praise to our beneficent Father who dwelleth in the heavens."

Since that day, each year the President of the United States issues the proclamation which invites the nation to give thanks for its progress under God and to enjoy the fruits of the earth which God has given them.

A very good modern Thanksgiving dinner can be planned using the same foods which were eaten by those who sat at the first Thanksgiving feast in Plymouth. We suggest that it might include Oysters Rockefeller, turkey with a wild rice stuffing, cranberry ice, and, of course, pumpkin pie.

Oysters Rockefeller

24 oysters
2 tablespoons butter
1 chopped shallot
1 tablespoon chopped parsley
salt
2 tablespoons minced bacon
½ cup spinach purée
bread crumbs

Arrange oysters on the half shell in a bed of rock salt to prevent their slipping while being cooked. Cream 1 tablespoon of the butter with the shallot and parsley. Place a little on each oyster and season with salt; then add a bit of the minced bacon and cover with some of the spinach purée. Dust with bread crumbs and dot with the remaining butter. Bake in a 450° F. oven for ten minutes and serve immediately.

Roast Turkey

Stuff and truss your turkey. Place the bird, breast up, in a roasting pan and brush all over, not forgetting the wings and legs, with melted salt butter. Dip a piece of cheesecloth in the melted butter and place it over the bird. Roast uncovered, at 300° F., allowing twenty-five minutes to the pound for birds under 12 pounds, and about twenty minutes for those that are larger. Baste with the pan drippings at half-hour intervals, removing the cloth during the last half hour of cooking. Season the bird with salt, pepper, and paprika when it is half done.

Wild Rice Stuffing

- 2 cups wild rice
- ½ cup butter
- 1 cup chopped celery
- 1 cup chopped onions
- 2 cups stock
- ½ cup sliced mushrooms
- ½ cup chopped green pepper
- 1 tablespoon minced parsley
- 2 teaspoons salt
- ½ teaspoon Worchestershire sauce

Wash and drain the rice thoroughly. Melt the butter and add the rice, celery, and the onion. Cook, stirring all the while, until the rice browns. Add the stock and the remaining ingredients and simmer for half an hour.

Cranberry Ice

- 2 teaspoons gelatine
- ¼ cup cold water
- 1 qt. cranberries
- 1¾ cups water
- 1¾ cups sugar
- 1 cup water
- 2 egg whites
- pinch salt

Soak the gelatine in ¼ cup cold water. Boil the cranberries in 1¾ cups water until soft and put them through a sieve. Add the sugar with 1 cup water to the cranberry pulp and boil for 5 minutes. Dissolve the gelatine in this hot mixture. Chill, and add the egg white stiffly beaten with the salt. Turn into a refrigerator tray and freeze for about four hours, stirring at half-hour intervals.

And, in memory of the land from which the Pilgrims came, we shall add one dish which New England inherited from the parent England:

Marlborough Pudding

12 tablespoons applesauce
12 tablespoons sugar
12 tablespoons white wine
6 tablespoons melted butter
4 eggs
juice and rind of 1 lemon
1 cup milk
½ nutmeg

Mix the applesauce, sugar, wine, and melted butter. Beat the eggs well and add with the juice and grated rind of the lemon and the cup of milk. Finally grate half a nutmeg into the mixture and bake in a moderate oven until firm.

NOVEMBER 30

Feast of Saint Andrew

It was Andrew the Apostle who said to his brother Peter, "We have found the Messias"; and it was Andrew who pointed out to Our Lord the lad with the five barley loaves and two fishes. Tradition tells us that Andrew was martyred in Greece, on a cross in the form of an X, a cross that still bears his name. Saint Andrew is the patron saint of Scotland, where his feast, known as Andermas, was observed in olden days by repasts of Sheep's Head.

Sheep's Head

Soak a well-cleaned sheep's head in warm water for three hours. Put it to boil with just enough water to cover.

When it starts to boil add 1 carrot and 1 onion, both sliced, 3 sprigs of parsley, 3 teaspoons salt and 1 teaspoon pepper. Simmer for about two hours or until the meat is tender. Remove the meat from the bones, skin the tongue, and serve both together. It may be served with an onion, caper, or tomato sauce.

Time-honored also is the eating of the Haggis, referred to fondly by the real Scot as "Himsel'," and by Burns as the "great chieftain of the pudding race." A leading culinary expert tells us "one does not attempt to make a haggis; one just buys a haggis and does not inquire too closely as to how it was made." If any of our readers is inclined to ignore this admonition, here is how it is done.

Haggis

1 sheep's bag	½ lb. oatmeal
1 pluck	½ teaspoon salt
½ lb. suet	½ teaspoon pepper
4 onions	½ teaspoon mixed herbs

Wash the bag in cold water, cleaning it thoroughly and soak overnight in salted water. Wash the pluck (liver, lights, heart) and boil for two hours in sufficient water to cover "with the windpipe hanging out." When cold, cut off the windpipe. Grate half the liver (the other half is not used), chop up the heart, the lights, the suet, and onions. Toast the oatmeal to a light brown and add to the above mixture; then add 2 cups of the water the pluck was boiled in, the salt, pepper, and the mixed herbs. Fill the bag half full, sew it up, and boil for three hours, pricking the bag from time to time to prevent its bursting. Serve the haggis very hot with mashed potatoes and boiled turnips.

Today Saint Andrew's feast is celebrated by patriotic Scots everywhere with ceremonies and banquets of less muttony variety—grouse and beef are more favored—but the Aqua Vitae which was the old Doric term for whiskey still plays a role. It is also a favorite day in rural areas of the homeland for foretelling the future by omens and charms.

In parts of England Saint Andrew is considered the patron of lacemakers—perhaps coming from the resemblance of intersecting threads in certain types of lace to the cross of Saint Andrew. Seventeenth-century bakers made cakes or buns known as Tandry or Tandrew "Wigs," composed of plain dough in wedge shape, ornamented with currants and caraway seeds. Also in England squirrel hunting was the traditional sport of Saint Andrew's Eve, and since the Andermas customs of England were also transplanted to the southern part of the United States where squirrel hunting is popular, we suggest a real

Brunswick Stew

- 2 cups dried lima beans
- 2 squirrels
- salt and pepper
- ½ lb. diced bacon
- 2 sliced onions
- 2 cans whole kernel corn
- 4 cups canned tomatoes
- 1 cup sliced okra
- 6 potatoes
- 1 tablespoon Worcestershire sauce
- 1 tablespoon sugar

Soak the beans overnight. Clean and disjoint the squirrels, dust with flour and salt and pepper, and brown lightly in a little fat. Place the meat, the beans, the bacon, and the onions in a pot, cover with boiling water and simmer for two hours. Then add the corn, tomatoes, okra, potatoes, Worcestershire sauce, and sugar and simmer for another hour. Mix a little flour with water and stir into the stew to thicken. Taste for seasoning and serve in a large tureen.

DECEMBER 6

Feast of Saint Nicholas

Saint Nicholas has been for hundreds of years a popular saint in the East and in the West, greatly famed as a worker of miracles. There are many charming legends concerning him. One tells of an occasion in heaven when all the saints came together to talk and to drink a little wine. Saint Basil filled the golden cups from the golden jug, and everyone was deep in conversation when it was noticed that Saint Nicholas was nodding. One of the blessed nudged him until he awoke, and asked why he was slumbering in such good company.

"Well, you see," he told them, "the enemy has raised a fearful storm in the Aegean. My body was dozing perhaps, but my spirit was bringing the ships safe to shore."

Saint Nicholas is the saint of mariners and also of bankers, pawnbrokers, scholars, and thieves! But he is especially the saint of children, and is known among them in various countries as Santa Claus, Kris Kringle, Pelznickel. There have even been invented servants to accompany him and to deal with the children who have been bad. Saint Nicholas is considered too kind to give scoldings and punishments, so, in Austria Krampus, in Germany Knecht

Rupprecht, and in Holland Black Peter go along with him, armed with a stout switch, while Saint Nicholas himself simply gives and gives.

Another very old legend tells us of the saint's kindness to the three daughters of a poor nobleman. They were about to be sold into slavery, because they had no dowry, when Saint Nicholas stole to their home and on three nights in succession dropped a bag of gold down the chimney. This is said to explain why three balls are the pawnbrokers' sign and why the saint drops gifts for children down the chimney.

Devotion to Saint Nicholas began in Asia Minor, where he was a bishop, and it was brought to Russia by an emperor who was witness to some of his miraculous works. It spread through Lapland and into Scandinavia, to other European countries, and finally to America. Up to that time Saint Nicholas had been pictured as a lean and ascetic bishop. In America, he became fat and jolly, and his miter was turned into a winter cap, his vestments into a snow suit. But he has kept his reindeer from Lapland, his propensity for chimneys acquired in Asia Minor, and the generosity of his heart.

A French legend tells that long ago Our Lady gave Lorraine to Saint Nicholas as a reward for his kindness to the world. He is still the special patron of that province and on his eve children hang up their stocking, saying:

Saint Nicolas, mon bon patron,
Envoyez-moi quelqu' chose de bon.

In Holland Saint Nicholas puts in an appearance on the eve of his feast. As the children sing, the door flies open and on the floor drop candies and nuts—right on a white sheet that has been spread out just in case. And after he has gone, there is hot punch and chocolate and boiled chestnuts served with butter and sugar. And in the morning, children find in the shoes they have set before the fire toys and many other good things—candy hearts and spice cakes, *letterbankets,* which were candies or cakes in the form of the child's initials, ginger cakes or *taai-taai* in patterns of birds and fish and the form of the saint himself. He also brings a hard cooky, called *Speculaus.*

Speculaus

½ cup butter	2½ cups cake flour
1 cup sugar	½ teaspoon baking powder
1 egg	1 teaspoon cinnamon
½ lemon rind, grated	½ teaspoon salt

Cream the butter and sugar, add the egg, and continue beating. Add the grated lemon rind and the flour sifted with the baking powder, cinnamon, and salt. Let the dough rest overnight in a cool place. Roll out as thinly as possible —about the thickness of the back of a knife blade. Cut into desired shape and bake at 350° F. for fifteen to twenty minutes.

In Switzerland Saint Nicholas parades the streets, his arms full of red apples, cookies, and prunes for the children who crowd to him. In Austria and Germany he throws gilded nuts in at the door while Rupprecht and Krampus, the spoilsports, throw in a few birch twigs.

In Poland if there is a red sunset on Saint Nicholas' Day, it is because the angels are busily baking the Saint's Honey Cakes.

Ciastka Miodowe (Honey Cakes)

½ cup honey	1 teaspoon soda
½ cup sugar	½ teaspoon cinnamon
1 egg	½ teaspoon nutmeg
2 egg yolks	¼ teaspoon cloves
4 cups flour	¼ teaspoon ginger

Warm the honey slightly and combine with the sugar. Add eggs and beat well. Sift the flour with the soda and spices and stir into the honey batter thoroughly. Let the dough rest overnight. Roll dough to ¼-inch thickness; cut

out with a cooky cutter. Brush with the slightly beaten white of an egg, press half a blanched almond into each cooky and bake at 375° F. for about fifteen minutes.

DECEMBER 7

Feast of Saint Ambrose

This is the feast day of the great fourth-century bishop of Milan who censured an emperor for his cruelty and an empress for her heresy, and yet who was known to be ready to listen to the woes of any who wished to consult him. Saint Ambrose is particularly remembered for his great charity to the poor to whom he gave away all his wealth. Among his own people of Milan, who even today boast of being *Ambrosiani*, the following story is told:

One day, although Saint Ambrose had increased the portions of meat he gave to the poor, so many came he found there would not be enough for all. It occurred to him then that if he had the slices of meat beaten flat and coated with nourishing egg and with bread crumbs, it would seem like more; in other words, his idea was what we came to call "meat-extending" in our own days of war-time rationing. On the pulpit of Saint Ambrose's great cathedral in Milan is carved the scene of a banquet of the poor in commemoration of his fine invention.

Saint Ambrose's recipe bears the name of *Costolètta alla Milanese*—which sounds much more poetic than the English breaded chops.

Costolètta alla Milanese **(Veal Chop Milanese)**

4 veal chops **salt and pepper**
1 egg **1 cup bread crumbs**
6 tablespoons butter

Have the veal chops cut about ½ inch thick. Beat the egg with one tablespoon water and season with salt and pepper. Dip the chops first into bread crumbs, then into beaten egg, and again into breadcrumbs. Melt the butter and fry the

chops for about ten minutes on each side—until golden brown. Serve on a hot platter with slices of lemon dusted with chopped parsley.

DECEMBER 24

Christmas Eve

No feast is so steeped in faith, in tradition, and in drama as this eve of the birth of Christ. Everything contributes to its dramatic qualities—the star-filled night, the angels and their message, the manger, the shepherds, the Eastern princes journeying from afar, the human family and the heavenly birth, the whole wonderful mingling of the material and the supernal, of poverty and wealth, of body and spirit. Even its smallest traditions lend themselves to the customs of the home.

Perhaps for this reason, because it is so definitely a dramatic re-creation in memory of this night, we speak here of the *Wigilia*, the traditional Christmas Eve supper of Poland. In the homes of that country, stalks of grain are placed in the four corners of the dining room, with a prayer for plenty in the years to come. Then bits of hay, symbolic of the manger in Bethlehem, are strewn beneath the tablecloth, which must be hand woven. The youngest child is set to watch for the first star of the evening, and when it appears he runs to tell the rest of the family. Then supper begins, as tradition has ordered it, with the breaking of the *Oplatek*, a semi-transparent unleavened wafer made in an iron mould and stamped with scenes of the Nativity. Each one at the table breaks off a piece and eats it as a symbol of their unity in Christ.

This is a meatless meal for it is a fast day. The number of the courses is fixed at seven, nine, or eleven. It is considered unlucky to have an odd number of persons at table, and relatives are invited, especially those who have no family of their own.

The soups are three in number, and always include *Barszcz* (a beet soup). There are three fish dishes—whole pike or carp, fish puffs, and salt herring; three accompanying dishes—homemade noodles with poppy seeds, red cabbage with mushrooms, and cheese *Pierogi* (dumplings).

Sandacz Pieczony (Baked Pike)

pike, left whole	1 cup cream
salt	1 cup white wine
1 onion	½ cup butter
juice of 1 lemon	

Clean and salt fish and cover with onion slices. Let stand at least one hour. Cover with cream, wine, melted butter and lemon juice. Bake at 350° F. for 30 to 45 minutes.

Kapusta Czerwona z Grzyby

(Red Cabbage and Mushrooms)

1 small head red cabbage	2 tablespoons butter
1 small onion, chopped fine	2 cups mushrooms
	2 tablespoons sour cream
salt and pepper	

Quarter the cabbage and cook in salted water for fifteen minutes. Drain, cool, and chop fine. Sauté onion in butter, add chopped mushrooms, and sauté for five minutes. Add chopped cabbage and continue to cook until flavors are blended. Add sour cream and cool.

Pierogi (Dumplings)

2 cups flour	½ teaspoon salt
2 eggs	½ cup water

Heap flour on a bread board and make a hole in the center. Drop eggs into the hole and cut into the flour. Add salt and water and knead until firm. Let rest for ten minutes in a warmed bowl, covered. Divide dough in halves and roll thin. Cut circles with a large biscuit cutter. Place a teaspoonful of filling on each round of dough. Moisten edges with water, fold over, and press edges firmly together. Be sure they are well sealed. Drop *pierogi* into salted boiling water. Cook gently for three to five minutes. Serve with brown butter and bread crumbs and sour cream.

Cheese Filling for *Pierogi*

1 cup cottage cheese	3 tablespoons sugar
1 teaspoon melted butter	3 tablespoons currants
1 egg, beaten	1/4 teaspoon cinnamon

Cream the cheese with the butter. Add other ingredients and mix well.

The Polish desserts for *Wigilia* are also three: a fruit compote made with twelve dried fruits (symbolic of the twelve Apostles), pastries shaped like horns of plenty and filled with purée of chestnuts, and a variety of cakes. Among the latter is

Mazurek

1 cup sugar	1/2 cup butter
2 cups flour	1 egg
1/4 teaspoon salt	3 tablespoons cream

Sift dry ingredients. Cut butter in flour mixture with a pastry cutter or a knife until crumbly. Mix beaten egg with cream and add to mixture. Mix lightly by hand and spread on buttered cooky sheet. Bake at 350° F. for thirty minutes. Take from oven and cover with fruit topping. Bake twenty minutes longer. When cool, decorate with candied cherries, angelica, and candied orange peel, and cut in 1 x 2 inch pieces.

Fruit Topping for *Mazurek*

1/2 lb. raisins	1/2 cup sugar
1/2 lb. dates	2 eggs
1/2 lb. figs	juice of 1 lemon
1/4 lb. nut meats	juice of 1 orange

Chop fruits and nuts with a hand chopper. (Do not put through a grinder.) Add sugar, eggs, and lemon and orange juice. Mix very well. Spread over baked pastry.

At the end of the Polish supper the numerous beautiful Christmas carols are sung and presents are exchanged between members of the household. In some places the remains of the *Wigilia* feast is given to the animals and bees and even offered to the trees on the farm, in the hope that all living things will prosper which have been fed thus on Our Lord's first night on earth.

In certain countries a Christmas tree for the birds is prepared, made of bundles of grain saved from the harvest and set on poles in field or garden. And in Scandinavia there is even a bowl of rice and milk put aside for the *Jule-nissen*, the friendly elf who lives in the attic or barn and sees that things go smoothly.

Animals are connected in many ways with the customs of Christmas Eve, for there is a widespread belief that they too must share in the blessings of Christmas. After all, did they not kneel to adore the Christ Child even before the shepherds came? Did they not, in fact, give Him the hospitality of their home when He first came to earth? There is a delightful tradition that at midnight on Christmas Eve all farm animals will be found on their knees; and that on that one night they can speak the language of men, to be understood, however, only by the pure in heart. An old English broadside depicts various animals and beasts with Latin inscriptions coming from their mouths. The cock crows, *Christus natus est* (Christ is born). The raven inquires, *Quando* (When)? The crow replies, *Haec Nocte* (This night). An ox lows, *Ubi* (Where)? And a lamb bleats out, *Bethlehem.*

There is not one country without its special dishes for this eve of Christmas, not one without its traditional food or drink.

In England for many years the favorite drink was the posset cup, a mixture of milk and ale served in a large pot, accompanied by a ladle. As the pot was passed to each guest, a goodly draught was taken by each, and with it was usually eaten a slice from a great apple pie. On this night "waits" or companies of carol singers went from house to house singing the lovely English Christmas carols. The usual ending, "God bless the master of this house," was the signal for coffee and cakes or a warming toast with hot buttered rum.

Hot Buttered Rum

1 lump sugar	1 jigger rum
boiling water	1 pat butter

Butter the inside of an earthenware mug. Drop in the sugar, fill not quite half full with boiling water, add the rum and pat of butter, and stir. This makes one portion.

Italy has its *Cenone*, or Christmas Eve supper, where fish figures prominently and a popular dish is *Capitone*, made with eels, usually fried. And Italian housewives prepare in advance for Christmas Day a sausage *ravioli* and the *panettone*, or currant loaf, so special to festival occasions.

In Greece Saint Basil shares the honors of Christmas Eve, when his cake waits ready to be divided at the evening meal. The first piece is cut for the saint, and then one for each member of the household. As each receives his share, it is dipped into a bowl of wine with the words, "This is for our grandfather, Saint Basil."

Armenia's simple Christmas Eve meal is fried fish, lettuce, and boiled spinach, because there is a tradition here that this was the supper eaten by Our Lady the night that Christ was born.

In Austria on Christmas Eve, every house is filled with the aroma of *Fruchtbrod* as it receives the visit of the *Anglöckler*, or bellringers, who go from place to place singing carols, sometimes two of their number impersonating Mary and Joseph seeking shelter at the inn. In Germany the Christmas observances go back to the start of

Advent, when a wreath is hung, usually from the ceiling of the living room, and to it a silver star is added each day, and each week a red candle. Also in advance is prepared the *Christstollen* (a long loaf of bread made with dried fruits and citron) as well as the *Lebkuchen* and marzipan, regarded as important holiday foods. On Christmas Eve the family gathers beneath the Advent wreath and sings carols. Then the Christmas tree is lighted and the gifts are distributed.

In Norway families gather around the table to partake of the *Molje*, a rich liquid in which the meats for next day have been cooked, dipping into it with pieces of *Fladbrod*, the hard Norwegian bread. And in Provence, we find a somewhat similar custom of dipping bread into the *Raïto*, a ragout made of a bewildering number of ingredients—onions, tomatoes, bay leaves, garlic, walnuts, thyme, rosemary, parsley, red wine, capers, and black olives, a wonderful mixture which has simmered for hours in olive oil.

In places all over the world, after the evening meal, people troop to the Midnight Mass that honors the birth of Christ. Some go through the snows of a northern winter and some through the gentler southern night, pressing into the churches, large and small, united, no matter what their nationality, in this night of the coming of the Child to earth; for the adoration of the shepherds began a continuity of worship which has never ceased. And in churches as well as beneath the Christmas tree in many homes thousands kneel before the Crib or Crèche—a representation, large or small, of the stable scene in Bethlehem, which received its inspiration from the good Saint Francis of Assisi.

After Midnight Mass in France, worshippers in the great cathedrals or in little village churches go home to eat the bountiful *Réveillon* breakfast, for now the fast is over and Christmas Day is at hand. The *Réveillon* varies between the city dinner with its conventional elegance of baked ham, roast capon, *vol-au-vent*, salad, cakes, fruit and wines, and the traditional country meal consisting of *boudin grillé* (grilled blood sausage), *pommes cuites au four* (baked potato), *vin chaud sucré parfumé à la cannelle* (mulled wine), or to put it literally, for culinary French is so delightful, "hot sugared wine perfumed with cinnamon."

The poorest in town or country may have eaten nothing but a bit of cheese washed down with *vin ordinaire;* but at least they will have "*réveillonné.*"

Truffled Capon

1 capon
1 lb. truffles
2 onions
salt and pepper
1 clove garlic
1 bay leaf
pinch of thyme
2 lbs. chestnuts
chicken stock
½ cup cream, or more
2 tablespoons sweet butter
½ lb. mushrooms
24 oysters

Singe and clean a fine fat fowl. Make a stuffing with truffles, peeled and sliced, the chopped onions, salt, pepper, 1 finely minced clove of garlic, a bay leaf, a pinch of thyme, and the chestnuts which have been boiled until just tender in some chicken stock and drained. If too dry, moisten the stuffing with ½ cup of cream. Stuff the fowl, spread with a buttered cloth, and roast at 325° F., allowing about twenty minutes to the pound. A half hour before the bird is ready to come from the oven, remove the cloth, and brush ½ cup of cream over it. Thicken the gravy with a little flour and add more cream if necessary. Strain and add the mushrooms which have been sliced and sautéed in a little butter and the oysters, allowing the sauce to cook only until the edges of the oysters begin to curl. Serve at once.

In many countries Christmas Eve brings with it the pleasant custom of the trimming of the tree. While the ornaments of today differ greatly from those of past generations, almost every family cherishes some of the old to mix with the new—the wax angel with wings that have been repaired again and again, the intricate colored balls, the glass icicles. Fortunately to be seen no more are the candles in their little snapper sockets, for these have given place to the safer electric bulbs. Well we remember the continuous agitation and the precautions taken in earlier days lest the tree catch fire. Our mothers always saw to it that the tree was set well away from the wall, and spent most of the time it was lighted circling about it watchfully, a cup of water in one hand, ready to put out any conflagration.

The origin of the Christmas tree is disputed. Some say it goes back to the Jewish Feast of Lights. In the days of the Druids, Saint Wilfrid is said to have asked his converts to adopt the balsam fir tree instead of the oak which had been the symbol of their former idolatry: "It is the wood of peace, the sign of an endless life with its evergreen branches. It points to heaven. It will never shelter deeds of blood but rather be filled with the loving gifts and rites of kindness." And when Ansgarius preached Christ to the Vikings, he referred to the fir tree as a symbol of the faith, for it was, he said, as high as hope, as wide as love, and bore the sign of the cross on every bough.

We know that in European countries in the late Middle Ages, fir trees were brought into the homes and ornamented with paper roses, apples, sweets, and gold leaf. Germany is usually credited with having had the first real Christmas trees, and they are mentioned in books as early as 1604. Prince Albert, longing for the *Weihnachtsbaum* of his childhood at Rosenau, is said to have brought the Christmas tree to England.

Just when the tree entered American homes is not certain, but it is surmised that the custom arrived with the Hessian soldiers in the British army during the Revolution. They set up and trimmed trees at Christmas as they did in their homeland, and the custom became widespread with the influx of German immigrants in the next century.

For the American family and the friends who gather today, either before or after midnight services in the churches, to trim the tree of Christmas, we suggest American refreshments of a piping hot oyster stew:

Cream Oyster Stew

6 oysters	salt and pepper
4 tablespoons butter	paprika
3/4 cup scalded cream	oyster crackers

Drain the oysters, reserving the liquor. Heat 2 tablespoons of butter, add the oysters, and cook until the edges begin to curl. Add the oyster liquor and bring to the boiling point. Add the scalded cream and season with salt and pepper. Serve in a bowl, topped with the remaining butter and dusted with paprika, and with oyster crackers on the side. Multiply this recipe by the number of portions desired.

DECEMBER 25

Christmas Day

The world's greeting for this blessed feast is "Peace on earth to men of good will!" It still rings out over the world today, as it did almost two thousand years ago in Bethlehem—a universal greeting expressing a universal hope. Even in lands torn by war and hatred, hearts remember these words and guard them for the future, awaiting the day when the bells of Christmas will once more, as John Keble says in his lovely hymn:

To high and low glad tidings tell
How God the Father loves us well.

Every country of the world has its time-honored customs for Christmas Day, but nowhere are they so heartwarming as in England. And, since our own ideal Christmas celebration is much like the English, we will put aside on this day the customs and food of other countries and deal exclusively with an English and American Christmas dinner.

"And did they actually eat the boar's head?" we asked a friend who was born and bred in England and knew its traditions. He assured us that they did, and also that the custom is still maintained there in at least one place—Queen's College at Oxford.

He told in this connection the perhaps apocryphal story of the origin of the boar's head as a Christmas viand. In medieval days a student at Queen's College was walking in the forest, studying his Aristotle, when he was surprised by a boar which rushed out from the brush to attack him. The student crammed his book down the animal's throat and choked it to death. However, he did not want to lose his treasured Aristotle, and so the boar's neck was cut off and the student's book restored. And since no one wanted to waste the head, it was roasted and eaten for Christmas dinner at the college table.

In the old days the boar's head was served at the very beginning of the feast, on a gold or silver platter befitting the dignity of the dish. Circled with bay leaves and rosemary, its tusks decorated with bright apples or oranges, it was brought to the table with stately ceremonial, attended by music.

The boar's head is still eaten not only at Oxford, but in other places in England, as well as in Brittany and in Central Europe. Should any modern reader be interested in the preparation of this "noblest dish on the board," here is how it is made according to the Vicomte de Mauduit who tells us how it was prepared in his ancestral home. The head was boned, leaving only the jawbones (to retain the head's shape) and the tusks. A stuffing made of minced pig's liver, chopped apples, a little onion, sage, and rosemary was used to coat the inside of the head. A second stuffing consisting of sausage meat, pieces of ox tongue, truffles, apples, mushrooms, pistachio nuts, and spices, the whole moistened with Calvados, was then placed inside the head. The head was wrapped in a cloth and boiled for eight or nine hours, boiling water being added as required. It was then allowed to cool and the ears, which had been cut off previously and boiled separately, were replaced in their proper position with small skewers. It is interesting to note that in modern England, when a boar's head is not available, a pig's head is used; and the meat cut up, mixed with various ingredients and boiled in a cloth. When the dish is ready, it is filled into a boar's head mould. Holes are left for the eyes and "these can be bought with the tusks from the supplier if required."

Another delicacy long associated with the English Christmas was roast peacock, also heralded to the feudal banquet table by special rites with music. In royal surroundings the peacock was not brought to table by serving men; but one of the court ladies carried in her own dainty hands the platter on which rested the lordly bird—"food for lovers and meat for lords." Its great colorful tail spread wide, its beak gilded, stuffed with spices and wild herbs, the bird must have been a fair sight and a dish of fine flavor.

Occasionally in a later England a little deception was practiced in the matter of the peacock. Washington Irving in his *Christmas in Old England* relates that he on one occasion looked with awe on the pie, decorated with the spreading tail feathers of a peacock, which covered a good bit of the dining table of his host. After a while the squire, whose conscience evidently bothered him, confessed that what was before him was really only a pheasant pie, though peacock should of course have been served—"but there has been such a mortality among the peacocks this summer that I could not prevail on myself to have one killed."

Of course, boars and peacocks were not the only outstanding dishes of the older English Christmas, for old accounts speak of a quantity and variety of special concoctions that leave us gasping in amazement. We may, however, mention in passing one of them—a famous pie prepared for a peer of the realm in an earlier century.

It is said to have contained, besides the crust, the following: four geese, three rabbits, four wild ducks, two woodcocks, six snipe, four partridges, two curlews, six pigeons, seven blackbirds; and it was served on a cart built especially to hold it!

Of the desserts traditional to the English Christmas dinner of early times none was more common than the plum pudding. The richness of its ingredients was said to symbolize the offerings of the Wise Men. Its rival, and sometimes in those heartier days its accompaniment, was the mince pie, alike endowed with meaning and considered on account of its shape, to resemble the manger bed of the Infant Jesus. We shall return to these desserts below, for, although the rare animals and fowl have been replaced by more usual and easily procurable fare, the plum pudding and mince pie are still prime favorites today.

The modern Christmas dinner ranges from elegance to simplicity, as the taste desires and the purse permits. Cookery books list menus in bewildering variety. But perhaps the best suggestions for a Christmas dinner are to be found not in a cookery book but in the pages of a novel—Charles Dickens' *Christmas Carol*, read aloud each year in many American homes on Christmas Eve, told over and over on radio and television. The famous Christmas dinner of the Cratchit family can be easily duplicated, and, with changes, offers a fine menu for any home today.

First as regards the goose—"that feathered phenomenon to which a black swan was a matter of course," described as served with gravy "hissing hot,"—we have given directions for its cooking on page 123. But here is a recipe for

Sage and Onion Stuffing

6 onions
2 cups bread cubes
1 tablespoon sage
½ teaspoon poultry seasoning
1 teaspoon salt
¼ teaspoon pepper

Cook the onions in a little water until tender. Combine with the bread cubes (the bread should be a little stale) and the remaining ingredients.

The potatoes mashed by Master Peter Cratchit, with what is described as "incredible vigor," in one of our families are served circled about with green peas; and over the white and green are laid strips of red pimiento—the traditional Christmas colors.

For the apple sauce "sweetened up" by Miss Belinda Cratchit, it should not be necessary to give a recipe, but here we would like to add a dish to the Cratchit meal—a salad or

Cole Slaw with Boiled Dressing

Remove the outer leaves and stalks of a small head of cabbage. Shred the cabbage and soak in ice water for an hour. Drain thoroughly before using.

Boiled Dressing

1 teaspoon dry mustard	½ cup water
1 tablespoon sugar	2 egg yolks
½ teaspoon salt	¼ cup vinegar
2 tablespoons flour	2 tablespoons butter
¼ teaspoon paprika	sour cream (optional)

Dissolve the dry ingredients in the cold water and mix thoroughly. In the top of a double boiler beat the egg yolks with the vinegar and add the dissolved ingredients. Cook, stirring constantly over boiling water until smooth. Add the butter and cool. When chilled, the dressing may be thinned with sour cream if desired.

We have come at last to the plum pudding—"like a speckled cannonball, so hard and firm, blazing in half of a half-a-quartern of ignited brandy, and bedight with Christmas holly stuck into the top." For after all there is no other such Christmas dessert. One could write poetry—in fact, many have—on this subject, and one could also rhapsodize in prose.

A plum pudding is, even at its simplest, a matter of many ingredients and of preparation far in advance. One of us remembers how it was made by an English grandmother. First came the buying of bowls, new each year and of various sizes, for many of the puddings were destined as gifts to relatives and friends: a big family got a big pudding, the small family a small one. Everyone was called on to help in the preparation, in the cutting up of the orange peel and lemon, the seeding of the raisins and currants. For this latter work the children of the family were pressed into service, and were offered an inducement: for every ten raisins the child got one for himself.

The ingredients were mixed in a vast yellow bowl used only for that purpose—very little flour but vast amounts of fruit and, to moisten, brandy and whiskey and ale. Over each white bowl went a new piece of unbleached muslin. The huge wash boiler was brought from the cellar, heaved to the top of the range and half filled with water. When it boiled, in went the puddings. There they tumbled about for hours, sometimes clicking against each other in their exuberance.

A few square inches of this pudding was all that even the most venturesome trencherman dared consume at a sitting. To us no other has ever tasted like it, not even the darkest and fruitiest plum pudding from the South. Grandmother Payne's recipe has been lost, but here is one almost as good.

Plum Pudding

1½ lbs. raisins
1¾ lbs. currants
1 lb. sultanas
2 lbs. sugar
2 lbs. bread crumbs
1 oz. cinnamon
6 oz. finely cut citron
grated rind of 2 lemons
1 oz. ground nutmeg
½ oz. ground bitter almonds
2 lbs. finely chopped suet
16 eggs
¼ pt. brandy
1 cup brandy

Seed and cut up the raisins but do not grind them. Wash and dry the currants. To the fruits add all the dry ingredients and the suet together, and moisten with the well-beaten eggs and the brandy. Butter and flour a piece of unbleached muslin, put the pudding in the cloth, and tie it up tightly. Put in a large pot of boiling water and boil for seven hours, adding boiling water if necessary. Remove from the cloth, pour a cup of warmed brandy over the pudding, stick a sprig of holly in the top, and set aflame as the pudding is being carried in.

Mincemeat for Pie

- 1 lb. chopped boiled beef
- ½ lb. chopped suet
- 1 lb. dried currants
- 1 lb. raisins
- 1 lb. citron
- 1 lb. sugar
- ½ teaspoon salt
- grated peel of ½ orange
- juice of 2 oranges
- juice of 1 lemon
- grated peel of ½ lemon
- 2 cups cider
- 1 cup brandy
- 1 cup sherry
- 1 teaspoon cloves
- 1 teaspoon cinnamon
- 1 teaspoon mace
- 1 teaspoon nutmeg
- 3 lbs. apples

Mix all of the ingredients and store in a crock in a cool place or fill into sterilized jars. If the mincemeat is to be used considerably later, omit the apples from the original recipe, and when filling the piecrust add an equal amount of sliced apples.

Dinner being over, both ours and the Cratchits', we might follow their example and group ourselves before the hearth to partake of apples and oranges and chestnuts roasted over the fire—and, of course, of the famous "compound." This was a mixture of lemons and gin and water made by Bob Cratchit, before dinner was ready, as Tiny Tim on his crutch stood watching beside him.

And we should certainly end the day, as Bob Cratchit did, with a toast: "A Merry Christmas to us all, my dears. God bless us every one."

DECEMBER 31

New Year's Eve

The last day of the year is the eve of the Feast of the Circumcision and in some countries is also celebrated as the day of Saint Sylvester. In Austria December 31st is also sometimes known as *Rauchnacht*, or incense night, for then the head of the home goes through the house and barns, carrying incense and holy water to purify them for the year to come. And in Rumania miracles are said to take place on this eve, for the gates of Paradise fly open and any wish made in faith is certain of fulfillment.

In countries where the feast is that of Saint Sylvester, much merrymaking and horseplay is connected with the celebration, even though the saint, the early pope who baptized Constantine, the first Christian emperor of Rome, deserves a better commemoration. Some of these German and Austrian customs for *Sylvesterabend* have been brought to this country. There is, for instance, the jest of the *elbetritch*, a mythical bird which the ignorant are sent out to catch in a bag; the unsuspecting person holds the bag as the initiates beat the bushes—of course, no one ever catches the bird. Many other customs concern the telling of the future on this night; in some places melted lead is dropped in cold water, there to assume prophetic shapes.

In Germanic lands the traditional dinner dish of the day is carp; guests sometimes ask for a few scales of this fish to treasure as symbols of good luck. A favorite on the menu for the midnight supper of this night is

Herring Salad

6 milter herring	2 stalks celery
1 cup red wine	2 boiled potatoes
2 cups cooked veal	3 sour apples
3 hard-boiled eggs	½ cup pearl onions
1½ cups pickled beets	½ cup sugar
½ cup pickles	2 tablespoons horse-radish

Soak the herring in water overnight. Skin them, remove the milt and the bones. Rub the milt through a sieve and mix with the red wine which should be dry and not sweet. Cube the herring, veal, eggs, beets, pickles, celery, potatoes and apples and add the pearl onions. Mix the sugar and horse-radish with the milt and wine and pour over the other ingredients. Mix thoroughly. Line a salad bowl with lettuce leaves and mound the herring salad in the center. Decorate with hard-boiled eggs, gherkins, anchovies, sliced stuffed olives.

Many heavier foods are traditional to the celebration of New Year's Eve in Scandinavian countries. A favorite dinner is roast beef, baked potatoes, *Risgrynsgröt* (rice porridge), *Lefse,* and *Kringler.*

Risgrynsgröt (Rice Porridge)

1 cup rice	¼ lb. butter
1 qt. water	1 cup heavy cream
1 teaspoon salt	1 tablespoon sugar

Wash the rice, drain, and cook in salted water in the top of a double boiler. Cook slowly until tender, or for about one hour. The water should be absorbed by that time. Add the butter, the heavy cream which has been whipped, and the sugar. It is traditional that one whole almond be hidden in the porridge and the person finding it in his or her dish will be the first to be married.

Kringler (Rings)

2 eggs	¼ cup butter
2 cups heavy cream	2 teaspoons baking powder
1⅓ cups sugar	2 cups flour

Beat the eggs and add a bit of the cream. Stir in the sugar and the butter which has been melted. Whip the rest of the cream until stiff and add. Sift the flour with the baking powder and stir into the first mixture to make a soft dough. Chill in the refrigerator. Roll the dough out thin, cut into strips, and shape into rings. Bake on a greased and floured tin at 350° F. for about ten minutes or until light brown.

On New Year's Eve in Greece singing groups, carrying replicas of the Church of Saint Sophia, go from house to house to collect food and coins; the model of the church is a symbol of the hope of recapturing Constantinople for the Christians. In Italy masked singers collect gifts of wine and money, of nuts and sausages; and at midnight go to the house tops to "blow away the old year."

The Moravians, after a love feast of coffee and cake, sing together *Nun danket alle Gott* to the accompaniment of trombones. In Helsinki the Finns formally greet the New Year with a concert on the steps of the *Suurkirkko*—the Great Church—whose bells peal at midnight and are answered by salutes from the whistles of the ships in the harbor.

As the old year ends, the Basques go in groups to the homes of friends to speed the old year and welcome the new. Their greetings are sober. "Who crosses this threshold enters his home," says the host. And as he enters, the visitor responds, "May peace be in this house." Within, a toast is drunk in hydromel or mead, that most ancient of drinks.

In the England of yesterday and today, New Year's Eve is celebrated with different forms of merrymaking and feasting, and the ancient holiday custom of the Wassail is much in vogue.

In our own country the observance of New Year's Eve takes many different forms—theater parties, dinners in cafés and clubs and restaurants; but we shall speak of two customs which many prefer.

The first of these is to spend the evening in one's own home with family and friends. For these, we suggest

Hot Mulled Wine

1 bottle red wine	rind of 1 lemon
12 cloves	2 tablespoons sugar

2 pieces whole cinnamon

Use a claret or Burgundy type. Pour into an enamel pot, add the cloves, the thinly pared rind of 1 lemon, the sugar and the cinnamon. Allow this to steep over a low flame, but it must never come to a boil. Serve hot.

An appropriate and traditional accomplishment is of course the fruit cake, for which recipes are legion, ranging from the dark brandy-soaked cake of the South to the delicate white fruit cake favored elsewhere.

Fruit Cake

½ lb. sweet butter	1 teaspoon salt
½ lb. brown sugar	¼ cup brandy
6 eggs	½ cup molasses
2 cups flour	½ cup sour cream
1 teaspoon cinnamon	1 lb. seeded raisins
1 teaspoon ground allspice	1 lb. currants
	½ lb. pecans
1 teaspoon cloves	½ lb. chopped citron
1 teaspoon soda	½ cup candied cherries

pinch of salt

Cream the butter and stir in the sifted brown sugar; add the egg yolks. Sift the flour before measuring and resift all but ½ cup with the spices, the soda and the salt and add to the butter mixture alternately with the brandy, molasses, and sour cream. Sift the remaining flour over the raisins, the currants which have been washed and dried, the broken pecan meats, the chopped citron, and the cherries which have been cut in half. Mix the fruits into the batter. Whip the egg whites with a pinch of salt until stiff and fold into the batter. Line two loaf pans with heavy wax paper, pour in the batter, and bake at 300° F. for about two and one-half to three hours.

White Fruit Cake

- 1 lb. sweet butter
- 2 cups sugar
- 9 eggs
- 1 teaspoon vanilla
- 2 tablespoons brandy
- ½ teaspoon powdered mace
- 4 cups flour
- ½ teaspoon cream of tartar
- ⅓ teaspoon salt
- 1 cup candied cherries
- 1 cup candied pineapple
- 1 cup candied citron
- ½ cup candied orange peel
- 1 cup pecans
- 1 cup white raisins

Cream the butter thoroughly and then stir in the sugar, again beating thoroughly. Add and beat in the eggs one at a time. Add the vanilla and brandy and the mace. Sift the flour before measuring and resift with the cream of tartar and the salt. Add the flour slowly to the other mixture and blend thoroughly. Then stir in the fruits which have been chopped, the broken pecan meats, and the raisins. Bake in 2 loaf pans at 325° F. for an hour and a half.

The second way of spending New Year's Eve may well be combined with the first: it is to attend watch night services in the churches. Surely this is the best way of all, to take time on this last night of the old year to reflect on all the joys and griefs of the twelve months past, to pray and plan for better things in the year ahead. Thus, beneath these New Year's resolutions may well exist the underlying hope that the new will be better than the old.

And what could better insure the fulfillment of such a hope than the prayers of countless people meeting in the houses of God on New Year's Eve, as the pealing bells ring in another New Year, their notes blent in harmony and not in dissonance, expressing what we all most deeply feel—the desire, as Tennyson says, to

Ring out the want, the care, the sin,
The faithless coldness of the times . . .

Ring out the thousand wars of old
Ring in the thousand years of peace.

Ring in the valiant man and free,
The larger heart, the kindlier hand;
Ring out the darkness of the land,
Ring in the Christ that is to be.

TABLE OF MOVABLE FEASTS

Year of Our Lord	Septuagesima Sunday	Ash Wednesday	Easter Sunday	Ascension Day	Whit-Sunday	Corpus Christi	First Sunday of Advent
1952	10 Feb	27 Feb	13 Apr	22 May	1 June	12 June	30 Nov
1953	1 Feb	18 Feb	5 Apr	14 May	24 May	4 June	29 Nov
1954	14 Feb	3 Mar	18 Apr	27 May	6 June	17 June	28 Nov
1955	6 Feb	23 Feb	10 Apr	19 May	29 May	9 June	27 Nov
1956	29 Jan	15 Feb	1 Apr	10 May	20 May	31 May	2 Dec
1957	17 Feb	6 Mar	21 Apr	30 May	9 June	20 June	1 Dec
1958	2 Feb	19 Feb	6 Apr	15 May	25 May	5 June	30 Nov
1959	25 Jan	11 Feb	29 Mar	7 May	17 May	28 May	29 Nov
1960	14 Feb	2 Mar	17 Apr	26 May	5 June	16 June	27 Nov
1961	29 Jan	15 Feb	2 Apr	11 May	21 May	1 June	3 Dec
1962	18 Feb	7 Mar	22 Apr	31 May	10 June	21 June	2 Dec
1963	10 Feb	27 Feb	14 Apr	23 May	2 June	13 June	1 Dec
1964	26 Jan	12 Feb	29 Mar	7 May	17 May	28 May	29 Nov
1965	14 Feb	3 Mar	18 Apr	27 May	6 June	17 June	28 Nov
1966	6 Feb	23 Feb	10 Apr	19 May	29 May	9 June	27 Nov
1967	22 Jan	8 Feb	26 Mar	4 May	14 May	25 May	3 Dec
1968	11 Feb	28 Feb	14 Apr	23 May	2 June	13 June	1 Dec
1969	2 Feb	19 Feb	6 Apr	15 May	25 May	5 June	30 Nov
1970	25 Jan	11 Feb	29 Mar	7 May	17 May	28 May	29 Nov
1971	7 Feb	24 Feb	11 Apr	20 May	30 May	10 June	28 Nov

Sources

Abbott, G. F. *Macedonian Folklore.* Cambridge: Cambridge University Press, 1903.

Alford, Violet. *Pyrenean Festivals.* London: Chatto and Windus, 1937.

Anderson, Robert G. *The Biography of a Cathedral.* New York: Longmans, Green & Co., 1944.

Anderson, Robert G. *The City and a Cathedral.* New York: Longmans, Green & Co., 1948.

Arnaudov, Mikhail Petrov. *Die bulgarischen Festbräuche.* Leipzig: Parlapanoff, 1917.

Arnold-Forster, Frances. *Studies in Church Dedications or England's Patron Saints.* London: Skeffington & Son, 1899.

Ashby, Thomas. *Some Italian Scenes and Festivals.* London: Methuen & Co., 1929.

Attwater, Donald (edit.). *Catholic Encyclopaedic Dictionary.* New York: Macmillan Co., 1931.

Auld, William Muir. *Christmas Traditions.* New York: Macmillan Co., 1931.

Bedier, Julie. "Stones for Bread" in *The Commonweal.* April 27, 1951.

Benedictine Monks of St. Augustine's Abbey, Ramsgate. *The Book of Saints.* London: Black Ltd., 1931.

Berger, Florence. *Cooking for Christ.* Des Moines: National Catholic Rural Life Conference, 1949.

Boettiger, Louis A. *Armenian Legends and Festivals.* Minneapolis: University of Minnesota Press, 1920.

Brady, John. *Clavis Calendarial or a Compendious Analysis of the Calendar.* 2 vols. London: Longmans, Hurst, Rees, Orme & Brown, 1812.

Brand, John. *Observations on the Popular Antiquities of Great Britain.* 3 vols. London: Bohn, 1849.

Brewster, H. Pomeroy. *Saints and Festivals of the Christian Church.* New York: Stokes, 1904.

Catholic Encyclopedia. Ed., Charles G. Herbermann and others. New York: The Encyclopedia Press, 1914.

Chambers, Robert. *The Book of Days.* 2 vols. London: the Author, 1863-4.

Count, Earl. *Four Thousand Years of Christmas.* New York: Henry Schuman, Inc., 1948.

Deems, Edward M. *Holy Days and Holidays.* New York. Funk & Wagnalls Co., 1902.

Dickens, Charles. *Christmas Carol.* Boston: Houghton, Osgood & Co., 1879.

Ditchfield, P. H. *Old English Customs.* New York: New Amsterdam Book Company; London, George Redway, 1896.

Douglas, George W. *The American Book of Days.* New York: H. W. Wilson Co., 1937.

Dyer, T. F. Thiselton. *Church-Lore Gleanings.* London: Innes, 1892.

Earle, Alice Morse. *Customs and Fashions in Old New England.* New York: Charles Scribner's Sons, 1902.

Englebert, Omer. *The Lives of the Saints.* New York: David McKay Co., 1951.

Englebert, Omer. *St. Francis of Assisi.* New York: Longmans, Green and Co., 1950.

Fehrle, Eugen. *Deutsche Feste und Jahresgebrauche.* Leipzig: Teubner, 1936.

Fergusson, Erna. *Fiesta in Mexico.* New York: Alfred A. Knopf, 1934.

Frazer, James George. *The Golden Bough.* 12 vols. London: Macmillan Co., 1911-26.

Friend, Hilderic. *Flowers and Flower Lore.* 2 vols. London: Sonnenschein, 1884.

Gallop, Rodney. *Portugal; A Book of Folk Ways.* Cambridge: Cambridge University Press, 1936.

Ghéon, Henri. *Noël! Noel!* Paris: Librairie Flammarion, n.d.

Greene, E. A. *Saints and Their Symbols.* London: Pitman & Sons, 1929.

Hackwood, F. W. *Christ Lore.* London: Stock, 1902.

Hazlitt, W. Carew. *Popular Antiquities of Great Britain.* 3 vols. London: Smith, 1870.

Henderson, William. *Notes on the Folk-Lore of the Northern*

Counties of England and the Borders. London: Stachell, Peyton, 1879.

Henry, Hugh T. *Catholic Customs and Symbols.* New York: Benziger Brothers, 1925.

Hogg, Philip. *A Calendar of Old English Customs Still in Being.* Reading: n p., 1936.

Hone, William. *The Every-Day Book.* London: Tegg, 1825.

Hone, William. *The Year Book of Daily Recreation and Information.* London: Tegg, 1832.

Hottes, Alfred Carl. *1001 Christmas Facts and Fancies.* New York: A. T. De La Mare Co., 1937.

Hough, P. M. *Dutch Life in Town and Country.* New York: G. P. Putnam's Sons, 1901.

Hutchison, Ruth & Ruth Adams. *Every Day's a Holiday.* New York: Harper & Brothers, 1951.

Irving, Washington. *Bracebridge Hall.* London: J. Murray, 1822.

Jameson, Mrs. *Sacred and Legendary Art.* 2 vols. London: Longmans, Green, 1874.

Karolyi, Alexander F. *Hungarian Pageant.* Budapest: Dr. George Vajna & Co., n.d.

Keller, Helen Rex. *Dictionary of Dates.* 2 vols. New York: Macmillan Co., 1934.

Klees, Frederic. *The Pennsylvania Dutch.* New York: Macmillan Co., 1950.

Koren, Hanns. *Volksbrauch im Kirchenjahr.* Salzburg: Pustet, 1934.

Lang, Andrew. *Custom and Myth.* New York: Harper & Brothers, 1885.

Larcom, Lucy. *A New England Girlhood.* Boston: Houghton Mifflin Co., 1890.

Laverty, Maura. *Maura Laverty's Cookbook.* New York: Longmans, Green and Co., 1947.

Laverty, Maura. *Never No More.* New York: Longmans, Green and Co., 1943.

Lednicki, W. *Life and Culture of Poland.* New York: Roy Publishers, 1944.

Le Goffic, Charles. *Fêtes et Coutumes populaires.* Paris: Colin, 1923.

Linton, Ralph and Adele. *Halloween.* New York: Henry Schuman, 1950.

Linton, Ralph and Adele. *We Gather Together: the Story of Thanksgiving.* New York: Henry Schuman, n d.

MacDougall, Allan Ross. *And the Greeks.* New York: Near East Foundation, n.d.

Marshall, Ann Parker. *Martha Washington's Rules for Cooking.* Washington, D.C.: Ramsdell, 1931.

Mason, Violet. *The Land of the Rainbow.* London: Hodder & Stoughton, 1933.

McSpadden, J. Walker. *The Book of Holidays.* New York: Thomas Y. Crowell Co., 1917.

Mead, William Edward. *The English Medieval Feast.* London: Allen & Unwin, 1931.

Menpes, Mortimer and Dorothy. *Brittany.* Boston: L. C. Page & Co., 1906.

Milburn, R. L. P. *Saints and Their Emblems in English Churches.* London: Oxford University Press, 1949.

Monks, James L. *Great Catholic Festivals.* New York: Henry Schuman, Inc., 1951.

Nickel, Markus Adam. *Die heiligen Zeiten und Feste.* 6 vols. Mainz: Kunze, 1936-38.

Omond, George. *Belgium.* London, Black, 1909.

Ormond, P. S. *The Basques and Their Country.* London, 1925.

Paddleford, Clementine. Articles in *New York Herald Tribune,* 1937-51.

Patten, Helen Philbrook. *The Year's Festivals.* Boston: L. C. Page & Co., 1903.

Pike, Royston. *Round the Year with the World's Religions.* London: Watts & Co., 1949.

Reichhardt, Rudolf. *Die deutschen Feste.* Jena: Costenoble, 1908.

Reinsberg-Duringsfeld, Otto von. *Das festliche Jahr.* Leipzig: Barsdorf, 1898.

Riis, Jacob A. *The Old Town.* New York: Macmillan Co., 1909.

Robson, E. I. *Guide to French Fêtes.* London: Methuen & Co., 1930.

Rombauer, Irma S. *The Joy of Cooking.* New York: Bobbs-Merrill Co., 1946.

Schamoni, Wilhelm. *The Face of the Saints.* New York: Pantheon Books, 1947.

Scherer, Margaret R. *About the Round Table.* New York: Metropolitan Museum of Art, 1945.

Schmidt, Friedrich Heinz. *Osterbräuche.* Leipzig: Bibliographisches Institut, 1936.

Sechrist, Elizabeth Hough. *Red Letter Days.* Philadelphia: Macrae-Smith.

Spencer, Edward. *Cakes and Ale.* London: Richards Press, 1897.

Spicer, Dorothy Gladys. *The Book of Festivals.* New York: Woman's Press, 1937.

Standard Dictionary of Folklore, Mythology and Legend. 2 vols. New York: Funk & Wagnalls Co., 1949-50.

Szalatnay, Rafael (ed.). *Old Bohemian Customs Throughout the Year.* New York: the author, n.d.

Treasured Polish Recipes. Minneapolis: Polanie Publishing Co., 1948.

Undset, Sigrid. *Happy Times in Norway.* New York: Alfred A. Knopf, 1942.

Varenne, Sieur de la. *Le Cuisinier François.* Lyons: Canier, 1658.

Vernaleken, Theodor. *Mythen und Brauche des Volkes in Oesterreich.* Wien: Braumuller, 1859.

Viski, Károly. *Hungarian Peasant Customs.* Budapest: Vajna, 1932.

Voragine, Jacobus de. *The Golden Legend.* Translated and adapted by Granger Ryan and Helmut Ripperger. 2 vols. New York: Longmans, Green & Co., 1941-42.

Wagner, Leopold. *Manners, Customs, and Observances.* London: Heinemann, 1894.

Walsh, William S. *Curiosities of Popular Customs and of Rites, Ceremonies, Observations and Miscellaneous Antiquities.* Philadelphia: J. B. Lippincott Co., 1925.

Warren, Nathan B. *The Holidays.* New York: Hurd & Houghton, 1868.

Watts, Alan W. *Easter.* New York: Henry Schuman, 1950.

Whale, J. H. *Patron Saints.* Ditchling: St. Dominic's Press, 1930.

Wright, Elizabeth M. *Rustic Speech and Folk-Lore.* London: Milford, 1914.

Index
of Names and Places

Index
of Food and Recipes

C

D

Lightning Source UK Ltd.
Milton Keynes UK
UKOW03f2210051216
289259UK00001B/23/P

9 780977 616855